MW01485034

THEY DON'T TELL

Child Abuse: A Mother's Perspective

Lisa R. Gray

This Book is dedicated to

Nikki & Tamirra

You showed grace, strength and courage where others who went

before you were not able.

&

In Memory of my Mom, Jessie Johnson.

A true Lady of Grace, Faith, Honor, my Friend

and Encourager.

You are deeply missed.

Acknowledgments

I want to thank Lynn Vincent, the author for her caring, encouragement, direction and kind words, you'll never know how you encouraged me to put on paper what was in my heart. Truly you are an exceptional spirit, and I thank you.

To my editors, Jessie Sanders, your expertise and help was invaluable. Thank you so much for your contributions. To Kim Glover, what can I say? Your skills and thoroughness, put the finishing touches where they were needed, you always had an encouraging word and spoke of the necessity for this work getting out. To Teri Klotz, thank you so much for your contribution to this project, for your encouragement with my writing when I felt like giving up, you boosted my confidence that I really could do this, and I thank you.

To my extended family from the east coast to the west coast, you have been there for us and we sure do appreciate you. We want to formally thank you for your help and for just being there for us.

To my Friday night Intercessory sisters, Diane Brabson, Joyce Snyder, I love you and thank you for your prayers for myself, my daughter, and my family during a very difficult time. My son Jared called it strategic, and I am in agreement with him.

To my friend, Evangelist Debra McNair, you put up with me when others had no idea how bad things were. Thank you for being there for us from the beginning. I love you and thank God he sent me a friend like you. To my Pastor, Carl E. Miller Sr. and First Lady Deborah J. Miller, I thank the Lord for your leadership and prayers for our family. You knew the Lord would be faithful through this and continued to speak life to us.

Thank you so much for continually reminding us of this fact. There were so many people who gave us encouragement; please know that every kind word, act, the flowers we received, the notes and cards were all appreciated. My family will forever be grateful for your kindness.

Lisa R. Gray

Forward

At a young age my mother heard God speak to her for the first time and began forming a personal relationship with him. It was clear that God had a plan for her life she just didn't know what it would be.

Her name, Lisa, in Hebrew means devoted to God. I can attest to that devotion through all the trials and tribulations. From being a single mother of three children, to uprooting your family from one state to another state, and being forced to change careers; it was evident and God was always the head of our household. My Mom was walking by faith and not by sight her whole life.

One thing my mother drilled into me and my brothers was no matter how bad your situation may seem God is in control and he is a good God. I'm sure at that time my mother never knew she would have to walk that truth on such a public platform. Yet and still she did it while holding my hand and showed me how to do the same.

During the time when the molestation was disclosed I saw my mother dig deeper in God than ever before. From the outside looking in it seemed like she had just become a Jesus freak, but now I understand that God was the only way to make it out and help others in similar situations.

I hope this book brings new understanding of what it's like to have someone you love be molested. It truly permeates all aspects of the life of the victim and everyone around them. The message we want you to know, understand, and believe is there IS a rainbow at the end of your storm and that rainbow is Gods promise to restore you to your full potential!

Nicole R. Gray

Disclaimers:

This is a true story, but some names have been changed to protect the privacy of some of those involved.

TABLE OF CONTENTS

1. My Story

For the Lord God will help me, therefore shall I not be confounded;
therefore have I set my face like a flint, and I know that I shall not be
ashamed. Isaiah 50:7 (KJV)

I am a mother, and my daughter, my baby, my precious, precious daughter, whom I love more than life itself, was sexually violated. She was used, abused, mistreated and had her innocence stolen from her while she was still a very little girl. She was only in the second grade when the abuse began, and it continued throughout her elementary and middle school years.

The Silent Crime. That's what sexual abuse is. It is the one crime in which criminals and victims individually and collectively keep silent, albeit for totally separate reasons, and it is this silence that perpetuates a world of abuse just waiting for the next victim.

What this book is not: This is not Nikki's story. This is my story. It is not an expose' of the abuse my daughter suffered. This is my story. This is my perspective, written from a mother's eyes, from a mother's viewpoint. I am not attempting in any way to put a voice to what my daughter went through. That is her story to tell, if and when she ever decides to do so.

Instead, I am putting voice to the heartache, the pain, the anguish, the shame, the hurt, the anger, the sheer rage, and the utter disgust I felt and still feel. I am putting voice to the utter disbelief that I, as a mother, experienced. I could not have known. How could I have brought the devil himself into my home to abuse my daughter?

How could I have been intimate with the same man who, with every chance he had, was abusing my daughter? How could this man who appeared to love me and my children introduce my pure and innocent, loving and accepting daughter to his perversion of sex? How could this man who played the organ in our church every Sunday morning fondle my baby and have her fondle him with every opportunity he could find?

I can't begin to tell you, to express to you, what the realization that I had been somehow oblivious to this abuse was like. There are no words. I tried to wrap my mind around it. I went into a place within myself I've never been before and have not been since. It was like a boxer going to his trainer's corner to develop their strategy for the next round. Because the truth of the matter is that is exactly what was taking place. Only my fight was not in the ring, and it was not natural. It was spiritual.

You see, I had taken an upper cut. I had been blindsided. I was on the mat and down for the count. Truly, the devil had his arms raised in victory, doing his victory dance all around me while I had a concussion and was in a daze. The cartoon stars were circling around my head, and the referee was giving me the final countdown as I tried desperately to figure out who I was, where I was, and what had just happened. I pinched myself, asking if this could be real. I couldn't sleep. I definitely couldn't eat. I went on a complete fast, no food or water for three days, knowing that the LORD was the only one who could help me now.

I did the only thing I could think to do. I hunkered down, called on a few prayer warriors and my pastor, and I went to see where I might possibly go from here.

Oh, sure, I still walked around in my body. I smiled and dutifully said all the right things. As a mother should, I told my daughter how everything was going to be all right, but I wasn't really present. I felt like an absolute zombie. I was the walking dead, walking around with nothing on the inside. I felt empty, no soul and no life. I had nothing. I *felt* nothing. My daughter had been raped over and over and over in her home, in the one place that was supposed to be safe. I thought this man was looking out for her! I thought he was protecting us both when, in fact, he was grooming us both, just so he could use her!

How low, I wanted to know, can a human being be? How filthy and how disgusting can a human being be?

And consider this. There is no way that a forty three-year-old man decides for the first time in his life that he wants to molest a little girl. He must have done this before. I simply had not known. I never would have married this man had I known his background. Sadly, frustratingly, maddeningly, somebody knew something. But no one spoke up. So my daughter and I each became another one of his victims. The silent crime struck again. Again I say that this is a crime in which the perpetrator and the victim both are silent, albeit for totally different reasons, paving the way for the perpetrator to move on to his next victim.

Prayer for the Author

Father God, I come before you right now asking that you cover me, even as I write this book, cover me as it goes out. God, don't let the enemy come in and make me ashamed that I've opened up and shared with these your women, mothers, daughters, people. I've done, O God, what you required of me, and I've done it willingly with a willing heart.

I pray right now God that you cover me, that you send your angels, God, to go before me and that you've made a crooked way straight. I just ask right now that you bless your servant, and that there will be no backlash from the enemy. You said in Proverbs the blessings of the Lord maketh rich and he addeth no sorrow. This is your servant's prayer in Jesus's name I pray. Amen

2. "Nikki Nicole"

But my horn (emblem of excessive strength and stately grace) You have exalted like that of a wild ox; I am anointed with fresh oil. Psalm 92:10 (AMP)

Nikki Nicole. That is the name her father wanted to give her, and I objected, "Tyrone you can't give her two first names!" I remember saying to him, so he relented and finally we settled on Nicole. We would nickname her Nikki.

Nikki is a kind, sweet, and gentle soul. She has a quiet personality, and she is very helpful. She has a positive attitude about life, and she has a unique wisdom that lets her see both sides of a situation.

Nikki is also a people-pleaser. She wants to satisfy others even if pleasing them is to her own detriment. She will do whatever it takes to keep the peace, taking a back seat to everyone else, with her own needs unmet. As long as those she's around are satisfied, she's happy. Her satisfaction comes from seeing others having what they want and need. She has very much the heart of a servant. Her joy comes from seeing your joy.

I've always known this about my daughter, and my concern was always that she have her own voice. I knew she needed to learn to speak up for herself, which was very difficult for her. I knew it, and yet I didn't really realize the extent to which she took that backseat. I didn't understand that she was SO giving that she would let others steal from her. I didn't realize she would allow a man to take from her what she had every right to keep for herself.

It was my job to teach her to do that, to teach her to stand up for herself, to teach her that she had every right to speak out. I did not do my job.

My dear, sweet daughter had been manipulated. Her innocence and pure love for others was twisted and used *against* her by her stepfather. That beast of a man took both the innocence and the loving kindness of a little girl and used them for his own prurient intent.

Every Sunday morning as I sat in church, I felt as though I was going through delivery. I would sit and feel the pain in my lower abdomen. Every Sunday just like clockwork, the labor pains would begin. I would get in the position and bear down until my insides, my inner being, could begin to feel relief from the devastation. It took great strength for me to deliver this baby, Sunday after Sunday.

For an entire year I went through these labor pains. Sunday mornings at church became my time and place of healing. These mornings became my release. My dear church family was there with me as the pains would come, and I would cry out in agony. They were there, Sunday after Sunday, as the tears streamed down my face. The ushers at my church were very kind. They thoughtfully had tissues always at the ready, and as I would bear down in pain, they would make sure I had something to wipe away my tears.

Isaiah 66:9 (ESV) says, "Shall I bring to the point of birth, and not cause to bring forth?" I'll never forget the Sunday my pastor preached on this topic. I knew that neither God, nor I would leave this work unfinished. I knew the frustration, the pain and the anguish had to end and that there had to be some hope of our lives being restored.

I knew it was time once again for me to assume the position and bear down in Spirit. This baby had to be delivered. I could no longer hold this pain; it had to be released. I had to be set free from this suffering. I knew I needed the strength it takes for a woman about to bring forth a new life into the world. It takes strength for her to deliver.

Prayer for Nikki

Father God, we come before you know with a prayer request specifically for Nikki. Father, I thank you for my daughter. I thank you for your covering of her. I also thank you that she has given me a reason to press on, to push forward. Lord, she makes me want to be a better person. I thank you for the heart that you've placed in her. Lord, I thank you that she still encourages me!

I'm truly amazed at how excited she was when I told her about this book for the mothers. I thank you that she no longer walks in fear, shame, guilt, hurt, or pain. I thank you, for your word will not return to you void, for surely you have restored her as you spoke to me. I wish for every mother to be able to say the same for their daughter. This is my prayer in Jesus's name. Amen.

3. Last Quiet Moments

My grace is sufficient for you, for my strength is made perfect in weakness 2 Corinthians 12:9 (KJV)

It was the Sunday after Thanksgiving in 2006. I was in the kitchen cleaning up, and my youngest son Jordan, was in the living room watching TV. These were the last quiet moments at the end of an uneventful Thanksgiving weekend before we went back to our weekday routines. I was teaching at a Detroit public school, Nikki was in the tenth grade, and Jordan was in the seventh grade. He was not very interested in academics, but he was getting by.

We were settling in to our new normal. I have three children. Jared is the eldest, now grown on his own and living in Maryland. Nikki came seven years later when I married her father and Jordan, my youngest son, came along a couple of years later.

I had finally gotten my ex-husband, Jack Reiss, whom I would later come to know as "the perpetrator," to leave our home. He had, until this time, refused to leave and had moved out only after a long court battle that had lasted an entire summer. In the end, he had relented, and our divorce became final in September. My divorce lawyer later told me that the divorce lasted so long because Jack was determined to continue to control me.

I had lost my father on July 2 of that year. We had lost one of our beloved aunts in March; and one of my best friends in May. The year 2006 was a uniquely unhappy and busy year for us.

As I put the dishes away, my daughter, Nikki walked up to me and said, "Mom if I told you something…would you be a mom, or would you be a friend?"

Her question hit a nerve within me. I knew I had heard that phrase from her before. You see, Nikki and I have always been very close. She has always talked to me. She has always known she could come to me. The minute I heard her say those words, I knew something was going on. My heart sank in the way that only a mother's heart sinks when she knows that something isn't right with her child.

I looked at her, at how timidly she stood before me, and I knew immediately that we had to talk, that whatever she had to say was not good. I went into the front room where Jordan was watching TV and told him that Nikki and I were going upstairs. I told him we were not to be disturbed.

When we went into my bedroom, I knew immediately that I would not allow either of us to come out of that room until she told me what was on her mind.

A Prayer for Grace

Father God, I pray right now, because truly your grace is sufficient. God, not only was your grace sufficient for me as I went through this, but your grace is sufficient for every mother right now. I pray right now that each mother will pull on, call out for, reach out for, and come to the Throne of Grace where they can find help in this their time of need. Let them know you are there waiting with open arms for them. Let them know, O God, you have not forsaken them, you do not despise them, you have not forgotten them, they are not abandoned, they are not without hope and without you, all the things the enemy is whispering in their ear is a lie.

You are there for them in this difficult time in their life, if only they would lean on you as never before. They will surely come to the understanding of what your grace can do in them, through them, and for them. If they will hold on to you, the author and the finisher of their faith. This is my prayer for your mothers, in Jesus's name. Amen.

4. Wouldn't My Child Tell Me?

No one really knows what is going to happen; no one can predict the future. Ecclesiastes 10:14 (NLT)

Years ago, I listened to Bishop T.D. Jakes a great deal, in fact, I still do. He is a powerful speaker and his ability to teach the gospel is truly something exceptional. Though, I always found myself thinking, "Why does he always talk about sexual abuse?" I know it happens. I'm not unaware. My head is not buried in the sand. I know it happens everywhere but does it really happen *that* much? I mean, does it happen enough to warrant him talking about it ad nauseam? I mean, really? Does he have to reference it as much as he does?

In my mind, sexual abuse was something that happened to others. It happened in the big cities where crime runs rampant. It happened occasionally in the little towns where a junior league baseball coach was trusted a little too much. It happened in the places where moms and dads were too busy to pay attention to what was going on with their kids. It did not happen in my town, and it certainly did not happen to me.

Boy oh boy, have I changed my story! Today I say, "Bishop, preach!" Today I understand that while I was thinking those very thoughts, I never knew that sexual abuse was happening in my own house, under my own roof, to *my* own daughter.

Sexual abuse. The sound of it is so ugly, so hideous, so utterly disgusting and distasteful. With those words come so many emotions, so many thoughts. Shame and guilt are the two heavy hitters, but they have some buddies: pain, low self-esteem, self-disgust, lack of forgiveness, rage, hate and anger. Not to mention the doors of access to degradation and manipulation. Then comes the downward spiral for the victim of abuse; the all-too-common cycle of promiscuity, teenage pregnancy, drug and alcohol use, and abuse.

The devil thinks he forever has free reign to wreak havoc in the lives of those who have had to endure the trauma of being sexually violated. That's why this thing is so hideous. The resulting horror of sexual abuse is like a game of dominoes; it permeates the lives it touches. It seeped into our lives and the lives of those people around us.

Prayer for Questioning

Father God, we come before you now once again to say thank you first for being our God. We love you, praise you, and adore you. Thank you for loving us. Now Father, we bring these, your mothers, before you who continue to ask the question, *why did this happen to my child*, over and over and over again. The enemy is tormenting them in their minds with that question, Father. So I ask right now in the name of Jesus that you stop the ruminating in their minds and you send the enemy on the run. No more torment! God, you are Alpha, you are Omega, the question that they will never have an answer to!

There is no answer to evil! Evil came in with the first sin, with Adam and Eve, that's when sin came into the earth, with Satan, the Father of lies...that's the answer to their question. The enemy, Satan, just wants to torment them in their mind and then laugh at his handiwork. Father, no more torment for your mothers! In the mighty name of Jesus, this is our prayer today for you. Amen.

5. The Elephant in the Room

Some trust in chariots and some in horses, but we trust in the name of the Lord our God. Psalm 20:7 (ESV)

The elephant in the room is a question which you may ask yourself a thousand times, or a million times, and still you may never get an answer to it:

Why *don't they tell?*

Why don't they tell?

Well, here is are some of the reasons, some of them are pretty obvious, others, not so. Some plausible possibilities:

- Embarrassment
- Shame everyone will know what was done to me
- Fear of the unknown... (Will it ruin their life?)
- Fear of the unknown...what will happen in the end?
- Fear of the unknown... will I be believed/supported or not?
- Fear of destroying the family structure
- Fear of causing a rift in the family
- Not wanting the perpetrator/family to be mad at them
- Too much of a hassle, I'll just leave first chance I get

Erin Merryn of "Erin's Law", a child abuse victim who has become an advocate for getting sexual abuse prevention education in schools states, "For two years I saw my mother cry, and so I put on a happy face and said 'I'm ok, this doesn't bother me.' I wanted to protect my mom because we hate seeing our parents in pain. It's that protective instinct kids have. Parents are supposed to protect their kids, but kids want to protect us, too."

Remember, this book is for mothers. This book is from a mother's perspective.

I'm not saying this answer is universal, and I'm not saying that this is always the case, certainly it is not. Yet what I am going to do is to offer up one possible explanation:

If you're a mother like me, you're scratching your head and saying…but WHY? Why didn't my daughter, with whom I have an awesome relationship, tell me? She knows I love her. She knows I would do anything for her. Why wouldn't she—why didn't she—come to me?

I don't know how you ever explain what is going on inside the head of a seven-year-old, but there is a scene in the movie *The Green Mile* where a crazy man is able to go into a home and into the bedroom of twin girls. He snatches them from their beds, keeping them quiet with the threat of hurting the other twin. The little girls stay quiet and are taken from the safety of their warm beds because of the love that each has for her sister.

You see, that could be what was happening in the minds of both your child and mine. My daughter may have stayed quiet because of the love she had for me. She believed I was happy with this her step-father. She was staying quiet for me.

"What would it do to my mom if she found out what this man she loves is doing to me?" your child may be asking.

So out of the love your daughter or son has for you, and out of the ignorance/shame/guilt of what is happening to them, they simply do nothing and wait for someone, anyone, to recognize their pain and their hurt. They wait for someone, anyone, to recognize that something is different about them.

They wait desperately for someone to see that something has changed. They are screaming on the inside. "Hey! Mom!" they silently cry out, "Can't you see? Can't you tell what just happened to me? Am I that good at putting on this false face? Do I only simply pretend like everything is the same and nobody will notice that nothing is the same?

"Look up, Mom!" they continue to call out. "Won't you please look up and see me? Won't you stop your busy life for just five minutes and notice me? Will anybody see this hole in my heart and soul"?

"Hey! Mom! I know you're running late for work, and I know you've got things to do, and I know the boss is riding you at work, and I know your co-workers aren't pulling their weight. I know your own mom is wanting you to do this and that, and I know the baby needs more diapers. I know you have to go to the PTA meeting tonight after school. I know we ran out of milk for cereal. But, HEY MOM! Won't you stop and hear my heart cry? Will somebody, anybody besides *him* pay attention to me? Don't I matter? What about me? Who's going to listen to me"?

"I'll just paste on this false face," your child says desperately to herself, "and go around in life like everything is okay, while on the inside, I just don't understand how you cannot notice.

"And now," your child continues, "finally I am at a point where I don't care anymore. I don't care if you don't notice. It doesn't matter. It is what it is and it doesn't matter. Everybody's a phony and a liar, and I can't trust anyone. Everyone around me—they are all just a bunch of fakes."

This becomes your child's story.

So why, oh why, oh why don't they tell?

This seems to be the question most people want answered, the one question that drives us crazy. We believe that until we have an answer, we won't be able to rest.

Why did this happen to my daughter/son? Why did this occur in my family? Why were we targeted? Why were we the victims of this horrendous crime?

While I would like to tell you that I have the answer, I may never have a complete answer. I may never have a full and total understanding of the ever-elusive answer to the question "Why?" The fact of the matter is that no matter the answer, it will never change the circumstances of what happened. It will never alter the facts of the crime. And it will never be enough to erase the harm that has taken place in your child's life.

The question of why is actually secondary. It truly does become immaterial. As odd as that might sound right now, it's true. At this point, the molestation has already occurred. It has happened and your child has suffered. The question of why is irrelevant.

Even if you were to find an answer, even if you were to have an unequivocal, definitive answer of why this happened, will it change anything? Will it change the hurt, the pain, the anger and the sleepless nights? Will it close the jar that has been opened? Will it enable you to go back in time and reverse what has already taken place?

My question to you is this: Why expend your energy on frivolous pursuits? Surely you need to conserve your energy for those things that are useful and productive. You *must* conserve your strength for all that lies ahead—for what you must now do to take care of your child and to take care of yourself. If you choose to chase your tail around in a circle like a dog until he gives up from sheer exhaustion, then okay, have at it!

I would rather you save the time and the energy you will most definitely need as you work—and it is work—to move forward. I would rather you take your time and energy to do something productive for yourself and for your child.

Although you may feel completely hopeless and defeated at this point in time, there is so much that you can do. Although you are feeling battered and beaten, although you may be at a loss, although you may be screaming "WHY?" at the top of your tired lungs, there are things you can do.

One thing you can do is to spend time with your child and together read self-help books on recovery. Nikki and I read *"Courage to Heal"* by Ellen Bass and Laura Davis. It's an insightful guide intended to help those of abuse come to terms with what they endured even as they work to move past their abuse with strength and with courage.

It is a book that brings both healing and hope to children of abuse and to those who love them. It's a wonderful chronicle that blends personal stories with professional understanding, as the two authors explain the 'why' of what happened and provide suggestions of how to deal with it. It's filled with the narratives of survivors. It's filled with compassion. It's filled with insights. I highly recommend it.

There's more you can do. You can be there for your child. I spent all my time being there for Nikki. On some nights we would sleep together. The more I was there, the more she was able to tell me.

Slowly, little by little, she was able to open up. She was able to shed some of her pain by telling me about it. Just as I have not been able to give you a full chronological account of what happened because it's too much, she was able only to tell me in pieces. She would tell me as she could, and I was there to listen. Be there to listen.

We also took a vacation during this time period. When we might have stayed to do all there was to do, to navigate all that had to be navigated as we worked to understand and deal with what had happened, we packed our bags and took a trip. We needed it. We needed to get away from the intensity of our lives. If you need to get away, do it.

We prayed. Oh, did we pray. Regularly. Together. Wherever we were. We prayed silently, and we prayed aloud. Those in our community told Nikki repeatedly how brave she was. They admired her strength for not hiding away in shame. They admired her courage because she refused to remain quiet as those before her had done.

You, too, can pray. You can pray quietly and out loud for others to hear. You can pray and pray and pray.

Prayer for Trust & Discernment

Father God, we come before you once again thanking for all that you have already done. Truly, God, you have been good to us; you have blessed us with an abundance, and we are grateful. Now, God, you said that without faith it is impossible to please you, so increase our faith.

Lord, it's our hearts desire to trust you more and more with every fiber of our being and our most precious gift...our child we return to you and say do as you please. Lord, you know what's best; have your way in my daughter's life, and I'll forever give you the glory, the honor, and the praise. This is our prayer. In Jesus's name. Amen.

6. An Overwhelmed Heart

When my heart is overwhelmed lead me to the rock that's higher than I. Psalm 61:2 (KJV)

The purpose of this book is to give support to the mothers. It's so important for them to know that they are not alone; that they do not have to live in, or journey through this darkness by themselves. They must know that others have gone before them and have survived. They've gone through the darkness and reached the other side. With the help of our Lord and Savior, Jesus Christ, you can too. You can lay the guilt and shame at His feet. You can end the never-ending questions, the confusion, and the wondering: *why did this happen to my child?* You can lay it all to rest and live in a future that is yet bright.

I want you to understand that there is still life to be lived—for you and for your child. There is a full life for you and for your family beyond the hurt and the pain of today. There is life beyond the circumstances of what has happened, even though for now, moving forward will consume a great deal of energy.

You have a child who needs you, still, to be a mother. Perhaps you have other children who need you. Perhaps you have a husband who needs his wife. At a point in time when you want to run and hide, when you want to shut yourself away from all you must do and dwell in the darkness, you must not allow yourself to do so. You must rise out of the darkness and trust that it will dissipate.

There is a way that you can do this. Trust me, I know how difficult this is, because I have been there. I have been so deeply buried in the darkness that I began to find comfort there. It was a place no one could reach me, and that was fine, because I did not want to be reached. There is a way to rise from the darkness; and you must be determined to do so because there are others who need you.

It is so important that you be there for your child. Even as you suffer your own pain. Even as you struggle to get out of bed each morning. You must be there for your child. You must tell her when she's wrong. You must encourage her when she needs it; and you must discipline her when it's appropriate. Please do not fall into the trap of feeling so guilty, feeling so much to blame for what has happened to your sweet child, that you abdicate your responsibility. You must continue to fully parent her.

If you are reading this because you are a mother, read on. If it is because you are a sister or a brother, read on. If you are an aunt, an uncle, a cousin, a trusted family friend, a loved one, a social worker, a prosecutor, a member of the clergy, a counselor, a friend of a mother whose child has suffered abuse, or simply someone who wants to understand a little more on this topic and the myriad of places it touches, please read on.

Please read on, as for the mother of a sexually abused child, it is a lonely world indeed.

If you decide to enter that lonely world and be a support to this mother, you will be entering a world where few have gone. Understand that you will only be able to go so far. She will be surprised, yet thankful for your concern, for truly she's on an inward journey that she can only take one step at a time.

Please don't ask a lot of questions. She has no answers. Please don't give a lot of advice. That's not what she needs right now.

If you choose to enter this mother's world to bring comfort and support, just let her know that you are there. Let her know that you love her, that you will pray for her peace and her return to wholeness. Let her know that you understand that *she too*, has been betrayed. That she is broken and needs a soft place to land. That she too, needs a safe place to talk about what she is feeling.

Make her see that you understand that, in effect, she needs to hear exactly what she's been so determined to tell her child—to hold her head up high, that she bears no shame or guilt. That had she known, she would have removed her child from harm's way.

Let her feel, through your kindness and support, the law of reciprocity working in her life. Just as she continues to be the healing balm her child needs, let your kindness and support be the balm that begins to heal the terrible wounds from which she suffers. As a friend and ally of this suffering mom, this can be your opportunity to give, to comfort, to soothe, and to support. This can be your opportunity to be there for her, to let her talk and scream and cry. To feel honestly, every emotion that she feels; and ultimately, to begin to heal.

Please do not ask this mom to be strong. She has no strength left. She has used every ounce of her strength to support her child. She has used only the thinnest stems of any remaining strength to continue in her role as a mother to her other children, as a wife to her husband, as a caring daughter to her own parents, and as a responsible employee in her job.

Perhaps God is calling you to be her soft place to land. Perhaps He is calling you to be her voice of reason, her sounding board. Perhaps He is sending you to do this for her because this is what she needs. Trust me. *This is what she needs.* She cannot continue to be all things to all people. She cannot continue to deny her own shattered soul.

If rather than being a friend to this woman, you *are* this woman, you need to know that "we," all the women who have gone through this darkness, stand on the other side, waiting to guide you through. We are here to be your great cloud of witnesses, cheering you on. When you get stuck in the dirt and mud of it all, when you decide it is too much to bear, when your family or friends no longer want to hear about it because they cannot understand, we will be here ready to talk about all that has happened. We will speak of it with all the wonder and all the disbelief as if it were the very first day of discovery. We are here to go the distance with you.

For we are a unique sisterhood. We will hold your hand. We will hold up your head when you want only to put it down. We will urge you to go out when you want to stay in. We will remind you that you have nothing to be ashamed of. We will whisper in your ear that you bear no guilt. We will tell you again and again: *you did nothing but love your child.*

So now you must love yourself enough to keep reading. It is the least you can do for me.

I ask you, are you ready? In Matthew 18:20, the Lord promised us that wherever two or three were gathered in His name, He would be in the midst. Know that even while you read this that you are not alone.

Are you ready? The Lord has breathed upon this work. Whenever you pick this up and begin to read, know that He is with you.

Prayer for Mothers with an Overwhelmed Heart

Father God, we come before you, because you are good, because you are merciful, because you are kind. O God, we just ask right now, that you'll be with mothers that have an overwhelmed heart. That don't know which way to go, that are just overwhelmed, God, with the circumstances they find themselves in. Father God, we just ask right now that you'll come right in and that you'll give them the peace that surpasses all understanding. And that you'll let them know that even in their circumstances you're with them.

Let them know that even though their circumstances may look bleak, yet if they will trust you, even in this, even when it's dark, even when they don't know where to turn, if they will just go to the Rock, and you are that Rock, if they will just not be moved by their circumstances, O God, that you will bring them out! This is our prayer today; give them the fortitude, give them the strength, give them the courage to get up, day by day, moment by moment, hour by hour, and move forward with the things that they must do.

Strengthen their hearts, O God. This is our prayer today, in Jesus's name we pray, Amen.

7. A Time to Process

Be careful for nothing; but in everything by prayer and supplication with thanksgiving let your requests be made known unto God. And the peace of God, which passeth all understanding, shall keep your hearts and minds through Christ Jesus Philippians 4:6-7 (KJV)

As I tell my story, I know it is hard to understand how difficult it has been, not only as I've done everything in my power to protect my daughter, but as I've tried to make sense of a horror that has penetrated our very existence.

You see, it is not only my daughter who was affected, but I too, am living in the aftermath of a disaster. I have suffered a type of major trauma and I was, in fact, I still am, trying desperately to cope with the emotional toll it has taken.

Although the pain is easing slightly, and a huge part of the healing has come from writing these words, I continue to live with a wide range of intense, confusing and frightening emotions. I know that only with time (much, much time) will I be able to clear the wreckage, ruin, and rubble that my world became.

My life was shattered. I was destroyed. I set everything aside so that I could help my daughter cope. I realize now that as I did all of that, I myself was not coping. I hadn't the time nor the strength to do so. I'm trying to cope now. I'm trying to understand. I'm trying to process. And I'm doing so by sharing my story with you.

As I begin to tell my story, I realize I cannot do so all at once. I cannot begin at the beginning and end at the end. I cannot give you an organized, chronological accounting of what happened. It's just too hard. It's just too terrible.

So I'm telling you my story, not as it played out, not as one event led to another, which led to another, but as I've come to terms with it. I'm telling you my story in pieces.

That's because I can only think in small doses about what happened to my family. I can relive it only in short sound bites, and review it only in the briefest of mini-film clips. I can read only for a little while about what other young victims of abuse and their families have suffered; and I can spend only a short amount of time studying the statics of abuse. It is all far, far too painful, still, to spend much time with it all at once.

When my story is done, you'll understand the horror. Perhaps you already understand, because it's your horror too.

As you share this journey with me, know that you're sharing it not as it happened, but as I have been able to process it. You'll find yourself peering into the mental processes of a mother of an abused daughter as she tries to come to terms with an unspeakable tragedy that touched her life and the lives of those she loves.

A Prayer for Peace

Father God, we come right now with these your mothers, we thank you, God, for your mothers. You honor mothers, you honored your earthly mother, so now we ask that you give your peace to these mothers which does pass all understanding, and because these mothers have come in and made the decision to get some help, some clarification, some understanding, we ask that your Holy Spirit come in and envelope them, O God, wherever they are, in their home, car, place of employment, in the courtroom, in the counseling waiting room, wherever they find themselves, if you would rest on them and let them know beyond a shadow of a doubt that you are with them, you will take them through this time. In Jesus's name we pray. Amen.

8. The Blame Game

May he strengthen your hearts so that you will be blameless and holy in the presence of our God and Father 1 Thessalonians 3:13 (NIV)

I so badly wanted to blame someone for what had happened to my daughter, and, as strange as this may sound, I was trying desperately to find the right person to blame. If only I could assign blame, if I could figure out who was at fault here and who should pay, then maybe it would all be okay.

I first, of course, chose myself as the most likely target of blame. How in the world does a woman live in the same house with a man who is molesting her daughter and not know *something?* Surely, I told myself over and over and over again, *surely* I should have seen something. I should have heard something. I certainly should have had some hint that this man I was married to was being inappropriate with *my* daughter.

I also wanted to blame Tyrone Gray, my first husband (Nikki's father). Had he only been faithful to me, I reasoned, I would not have divorced him. I would not have loaded up the kids and left Maryland. Tyrone had LOVED Nikki. He adored her as a father should. He never would have molested her. Had he been a faithful husband to me, I never would have left him, I never would have been with Jack ergo, Nikki would never have been molested.

I also spent a little time thinking I might blame Tyrone's new wife. She had known he was married to me, but she shamelessly chased him anyway. She would come to our marital home looking for him, not caring that he had wife—that he had children. In my desperate need to blame someone, anyone, for what had happened to my daughter, this woman made an obvious and excellent villain for the saga playing out in our lives. She could easily be named the culprit. At least my head was telling me so.

I also wanted to blame my sweet baby girl, Nikki. How could she not tell me what this pervert had done? How could she not tell me the horrible things that were being done to her? Well, okay, I told myself, yes, she was a child at the time. But, I continued to argue with the part of me so desperate to assign blame, and I said, *she is not a child anymore*. Why didn't she tell me once she was big enough to understand what was happening?

There had been so many years, so many chances for her to tell me. How many different opportunities had there been? She could have said *something*. Or why didn't she, at the very least, tell her best friend, Kayla? All these years. Surely she would have told *Kayla*! But even as I wanted to blame Nikki, I knew I couldn't do so. That would be blaming the victim. I can't, I reminded myself, I simply won't go there.

When I couldn't find the proper scoundrel at whom I could boldly point my finger, I expanded my search. I turned to Jack's family. His family, I deduced, must have known what this depraved man was doing! They knew him. They must have at least suspected something. But they refused to speak out. They, of course, did not/would not speak out against for their brother/son/uncle.

So I thought, what about his friends then? They know what type of a person he is. They know that he is a liar. They, I was certain, were covering for him. They certainly had seen something. They absolutely must have known something. And yet, just as all the others he had buffaloed, they did not say a word.

I knew in my heart of hearts that there had been other victims that Jack had done this all before. Had these earlier victims spoken up, this would not have happened to my daughter. Had they told someone—anyone—what Jack had done to them, surely Nikki

31

would have been saved. She would not have been violated. She would not be suffering this shame.

Finally there was the community at large. We lived in a small city with an even smaller community of blacks. We know everyone. Everyone knows us. Someone, certainly, knew something about Jack and his perversity. Someone knew, but that someone never bothered to tell. Had they only told, another child would not have been exploited at his hands.

I so very desperately wanted to find someone to blame for what had happened to my daughter, what had happened to all of us. I still do. But in the end reason steps in, and I know there really is only one person on whom I can place this blame. And that person is Jack Reiss, Jack, the adult who secretly, methodically and deliberately colluded to molest an innocent little girl and to hide this fact with every opportunity he had.

Prayer for the Perpetrator

Father God, in the name of Jesus we come before you now, asking that you would do that which only you can do, and that is change hearts. Lord, change the heart of a man that would want to harm one of your children. Lord, change the heart of a man that would chose to molest a child.

Lord, I ask that you go in and do a work, an inside job, O Lord; only you can do that, and if you do, we will forever give you the praise, the honor and the glory; we'll tell somebody about you, Father. In the name of Jesus we pray. Amen.

9. Heart of Flesh

A new heart also will I give you, and a new spirit will I put within you: and I will take away the stony heart out of your flesh, and I will give you a heart of flesh. Ezekiel 36:26 (KJV)

One of my earliest prayers and my prayer for you is to have a "Heart of Flesh." I wanted desperately to continue to be loving, giving and caring. I wanted to remain open and alive. I did not want to become harsh or cold or closed off, even though the circumstances encouraged it—even though I could and you could so easily justify bitterness. In the end the only person that would be hurt if we changed who we really are and began to live our lives out of the bitterness, out of our anguish would be ourselves.

We know this scourge of child molestation is happening throughout this country. It is affecting untold numbers of little girls and boys, which means there are untold numbers of mothers, stretching from the east coast of New Hampshire to the west coast of California; spanning from the mountains of Montana to the southernmost Keys of Florida. All walking around with the guilt and the shame that accompanies having this horror happen to their child; and most are suffering in silence. Most feel that there is no one to talk to. Most feel that there is nowhere to turn.

If you are one of these mothers, your first concern, and rightfully so, is for your child. Resources for a sexually abused child are plentiful and accessible. If you are reading this book and have a child that has been molested, you most likely have accessed some, if not many, of those resources. If you haven't, do so immediately. Put this book down and make some phone calls. Find your child the help he or she needs.

You are now at the point where most mothers who have lived through this horror find themselves. These mothers have gotten the child the help needed, but they have had to come back to their home alone. They are left to deal with their own horrors. They must find a way to cope with the guilt and shame and sleeplessness. They must find a way to quiet the wondering and ruminating. They must learn to live with the questions: How could this have happened? How could I not see it? Am I blind? Am I stupid? What kind of mother am I that my child wouldn't tell me?

The horror of all the thoughts this mother cannot quiet goes on. Minute after minute, hour after hour, day after day, and week after week. It goes on for months and, for some, years. It has been nine years since my daughter disclosed her truth to me and still, from time to time, I am haunted by the question: How could this have happened?

In many ways, a mother of an abused child is silenced. Her primary concern, of course, is the well-being of her child. Yet no one knows the extent of what *she* has to go through. No one sees the emotional hell she must endure.

A Mother's Prayer

Lord, you have answered every prayer I have prayed about this. You have restored my daughter just like you said you would. You have given victory in the trial. You have let those girls and women who did not, because they could not, speak out against this abuser feel vindicated with this finding of guilt on the part of the jury. There is one prayer yet to be answered in this regard, and that is for Jack Reiss to admit to his family, friends, community and most of all to you Lord what he did to Nikki, Tamirra, and the countless other victims, including his relatives. My expectation is by the time this book is completed, Lord, You will have answered that prayer as well.

Now Father for those Mothers who decide not to take the Perpetrator to trial for whatever reason I pray Father that they have peace in their decision, it is such a personal decision, Father grant them the peace that surpasses all understanding, and Father should they decide not to speak up, cause that Perpetrator not to touch another child, don't let another child fall victim, because someone didn't speak up and let it be known there was a wolf amongst the sheep.

Father we also pray for those children and Mothers that go to trial and for whatever reason are not victorious in the court system, maybe because of a slick defense attorney, a ill-equipped prosecutor, some rule of law that goes in the defenses favor, or any number of reasons, Father we ask right now for your covering in those instances as well that you will cause the child, the Mother, the family to know that did the right thing when they took a stand against evil.

When they stood up and said this was not right what happened to me. Lord we pray right now that you will cause the children to know that you are with them through every situation and that YOU are there vindicator, sometimes vindication is sudden, sometimes, it's slow, but the truth will always STAND in the end, it will not lie. This is our prayer in Jesus name we pray. Amen

10. Suffering in Silence

Come to me, all who labor and are heavy laden, and I will give you rest.[29] Take my yoke upon you, and learn from me, for I am gentle and lowly in heart, and you will find rest for your souls.[30] For my yoke is easy, and my burden is light. Matthew 11:28-30 (ESV)

The first time someone recognizes your pain is like a breath of fresh air. My hope and prayer for this book and for the untold number of mothers who are suffering is that it be like a breath of fresh air. My hope and prayer is that you feel a recognition of your pain and can find renewal in the validation that such recognition brings. For every child abuse victim, there is a family that also must pick up the pieces and cope with the abuse.

Oftentimes when you are suffering, you wear a mask. You faithfully pick up that secret mask each and every day and put it on so that you can go about your business—so that you can get things done without everyone around you pointing you out: there's the woman who suffered such pain. You put it on so that you can accomplish life, so that you can do what need to be done. But the mask cannot hide the pain from you. You're still suffering. And there is a part of you which needs to be recognized. There's a part of you yearning to be acknowledged. There's a part of you that so desperately needs to be validated.

Because you're hiding secretly away behind your mask, however, the recognition, the acknowledgement, the validation doesn't come. And when it doesn't, a part of you—I should say *another* part of you—dies.

The psyche is multifaceted, like a diamond with many beautiful surfaces. The brilliance of these many angles shines as you twist and turn, and the psyche shows off all its beautifully intriguing sides. So you do, too; you shine with many beautiful prisms as the person who embodies this psyche. You have many facets, many roles and personas, that must be fulfilled.

As the mother of a child abused, you are fulfilling so many roles. You are taking care of your child. First, foremost and always, you are guardian and protector and fierce lioness protecting her vulnerable cub. However, that is not all you are—even as you snarl and lash out at anyone who might continue to do your child harm.

You are also still you. You, too, have been hurt. You, too, have suffered. But hiding behind your mask, you suffer in silence. There is no one there to peek behind the mask and offer you the acknowledgment and the validation that you need. There is no one there to witness the damage *you* have suffered—the damage you continue each and every day to suffer.

Your suffering is certainly not something which you voice. The damage you've endured is certainly not something you mention to others. When your child has been molested, your concern is for her recovery. Your pain, however real and strong and debilitating it is, goes silently unseen.

My own experience, as well as my contact with other mothers who have undergone this trauma firsthand, tells me that all the mothers out there—all the mothers who have had to deal and are dealing with this today—too, are suffering. They are suffering from the results of trauma and are in need of specialized services. They need help, which is *not* being offered. Their pain is in no way being recognized. It is not being acknowledged.

It is also my belief that on some level many of these moms themselves may not know, or perhaps may be in denial, of their own need. Anyone dealing with trauma knows that the first stage after experiencing it is shock, which hinders the ability to call for help. When you are in shock, you are not in a position to reach out for assistance for yourself.

Immediately after suffering a trauma is a vital time when those around you may need to come to your aid. You are too traumatized to help yourself, so you must rely on your loved ones, your family, your friends and/or your clergy. If you are already in the legal system, which can be traumatic all by itself, the professionals there would be wise to recommend specialized services for both the victim and for you, the caregiver.

There were a few times when I felt especially validated during this process, and a few times when I felt especially invisible. After the trial, after Jack had been found guilty, there was an opportunity for me to give a *victim impact statement*.

Nikki could give a statement and, as her mother, so could I. And I did. I took my time preparing my statement, which ended up being rather lengthy—about ten pages. I spent a lot of time putting thought into the IMPACT of what had transpired, how it had impacted, how it had affected, my daughter, me, and my family. The prosecutor, who had been absolutely wonderful during the entire pre-trial and trial process, to my dismay, discounted my statement. She asked me to shorten it GREATLY.

Fortunately, however, Tamirra's caseworker, Candy, said to me, "You need to have a voice in what this has done to you, too!"

Hearing those words come out of her mouth was so refreshing for me. It felt so good to know that I mattered. Yes, I could make a difference too. Yes, I had been violated too. Yes, this horrible thing that my daughter had suffered impacted my life too. I'll forever be grateful to her for that. That acknowledgment, that validation of my hurt—of my pain and my agony—was a turning point in my being able to let go of some of my anxiety and of the indignation I'd so firmly held on to.

It is exactly the lack of this type of validation that needs to be addressed by the professionals who want to help both the children who are victims of abuse and their parents. Not all professionals are as insightful as was Tamirra's caseworker.

Not all professionals understand the aftermath of you, as a parent, learning that your child—YOUR CHILD, the child you would die to protect—has been sexually abused.

First there is shock; and then comes disbelief. Both are followed by anger, by sorrow, even by ambivalence, as you are not sure what to think or what to feel. All are typical and VALID responses to hearing your child say that he or she has been abused; and when the abuse has come at the hands of someone close to you—a family member, perhaps—then there is the overwhelmingly painful sense of betrayal. It is deep and profound. It cuts to the very core.

It is absolutely essential for professionals working with families in these situations to discover the effect of a child's abuse on the child's parents or caregivers. Understanding what the parent's experience, what they go through and how they suffer, is critical in providing them the help they need. And trust me when I say this, because I was them.

It is also absolutely essential for everyone to understand that there is no single "right" or "wrong" way for parents to deal with hearing that their child has been sexually molested. Just as we all cope with different situations in different ways, parents react differently. And that's okay. That doesn't mean that one parent is more caring than another. It doesn't mean that one parent could be at fault while another probably isn't. It is only in the asking of questions and the listening to answers that there can be an understanding of what these non-offending parents need in terms of support.

It is essential that our society begin to understand that helping the parents of molested children is *critical* After all, the parent is the one to whom the child will continue to turn. The parent will be the one helping to pick up the pieces long after the professionals have clocked out for the day.

Prayer for Suffering

Father God, in the name of Jesus we come to you on behalf of your suffering mothers, Father. Father, you are the God of all comfort, and you said you would comfort us in all our tribulation so we may be able to comfort others who are in trouble. Father, you know their hearts cry; Father, you know those unspoken desires, fears, and concerns.

Father, we ask right now in the name of Jesus that you would not only comfort but you would also reassure these your mothers that you have not forsaken them during this their great time of need. Father, you will give them the strength they need in the inner man, the peace they need, the wisdom they need to make the right decisions for themselves, their daughters, and their family.

Father, you said in your word that many are the afflictions of the righteous but you would deliver us out of them all if we trust in you. This is our prayer in Jesus's name. Amen.

11. Post-Traumatic Stress

Make me to hear joy and gladness; Psalm 51:8 (KJV)

Just as your daughter has suffered immensely, so have you. Just as your daughter must talk, so must you.

What you have suffered goes beyond anything you might ever have imagined. Never in your wildest dreams did you think such a thing could happen to *your* daughter. Equally, the impact of this trauma, because it is indeed a trauma, goes far beyond anything you've ever had to endure.

It resonates from within your very core, causing an emotional toll that only you can describe. In fact, you may not be able to describe it at all. The pain, confusion and fear are so horrible, so strong, that perhaps you cannot say anything at all. There are no words to explain the giant ball of nerves threatening to crush you. It's important that you realize it will take time to overcome the stress and the anguish threatening to destroy you. It will take some time to regain your emotional balance.

With understanding and with patience, however, you will survive.

The understanding comes not from knowing *why* this happened. You may never come to terms with that. There is no coming to terms with why the devil himself chose you and your daughter for his destruction. There may never be a true understanding of why he entered your life and shattered your world, leaving you vulnerable and powerless, at least for a while, against him. The understanding, instead, comes from *accepting* that this has happened. It comes from knowing that your anxiety, your fear, and your uncertainty are okay. These emotions are normal and to be expected. It is only with feeling them and then dealing with them that you, your daughter, and your life can return to normal.

As you work to process what has happened, just as I continue to do every single day of my life—as I've continued to struggle to do for the past seven years—you can begin to accept the reality that you have suffered and that you must find a way to cope with your suffering if you are once again to find your life.

One way to begin to cope with what has happened is to know that there is no absolute right or wrong way to feel. You are going to think and respond the way you do. Second-guessing your reactions, demanding from yourself that you act a certain way or that you *be* a certain way, is not what you should do. Be kind to yourself. Be patient with and tolerant of yourself. Remind yourself—and this is so important—that you're doing the best you can. You already feel such guilt for what has happened. Do not let yourself feel guilt for your response to it. Kick, scream, yell, hide under the covers for a week, take a vacation, eat chocolate, and hate the predator and all he stands for. Do whatever it is you need or want to do. It's okay. Do not demand that you think or feel a certain way. Think and feel the way you think and feel.

You may find yourself shaking. You may suddenly feel yourself trembling from the inside out. Your stomach may tighten and churn.

While going into the grocery on just another Monday, you may find your heart pounding out of your chest. With a lump in your throat, you might realize you are breathing at three times the normal rate. You might break out in a cold sweat and feel dizzy or faint. Through it all, your thoughts may race. This is called anxiety. It is a normal reaction to stress.

In reality, not acknowledging your true feelings will impede the healing that must be done. Sure, it may seem better to go into denial. Trying not to experience what you're feeling, however, will not make those feelings disappear. Even if you desperately try to ignore them, they do and will continue to exist. Allowing yourself to feel them, with all the horror and pain and frustration that accompany them, will eventually reduce their power. And when the feelings and the memories have less power, the accompanying horror, pain and frustration can finally begin to fade.

Some mothers who've gone through this are purposefully determined to hold onto the pain. That, too, is understandable. They fear that by letting go of their feelings they are denying the shame and guilt that is rightfully theirs. Please understand that that's okay as well. This has been the most horrendous event that any one of us can imagine. Your precious baby has been abused. And you did nothing to stop it.

Remember that you did nothing to stop it because *you did not know*. Had you known, you would have done anything, you would have done everything, to stop it. You simply did not know. And now you do. Now you must learn to cope with it. For your daughter. And for yourself.

If you can, talk about what you're feeling. You've encouraged your daughter to talk. You know she must talk if she is going to heal, if she is going to be able to live a life that is full and happy and normal. You, too, if you're going to heal, if you're going to live a life that is full and happy and normal, must talk.

Yes. It's hard to face those feelings. It's even harder to express them. But doing so is essential. If you have a friend, a shoulder to cry on, do so. If not, find another way to get those feelings out. You might journal or paint or craft or even pound them out onto the pavement as you run. Just do something to get them out. If you don't, they can and will grow. And then they can and will bury you.

As you struggle to cope with the trauma, because that truly is what it is, you will experience a wide array of reactions, both emotional and physical. You will be nervous and anxious and jumpy. At other times, you will be numb. You'll feel completely disconnected to the world around you.

Feeling a sense of disbelief and shock, is to be expected. The reality of what has happened is beyond belief. But it happened. Feeling a sense of fear is also to be expected—fear that this could happen again—fear that you cannot protect your family.

Certainly you'll be sad. You'll be sad for your daughter and what she has had to endure. You'll be sad for a society that is so insidiously infected with beasts who perpetuate this crime.

You may, too, feel absolutely helpless. With no warning, with no advanced notice whatsoever, the devil entered your home and took advantage of your daughter. Being the victim of such a violent, sudden, unforeseen attack will surely leave you with a sense of vulnerability.

Then there's the guilt, the anger, and the shame. These are all natural, normal reactions to what you have been through. Allow yourself to feel them. Allow yourself to feel whatever you feel. Eventually, and it may take a long, long time, but eventually you and your daughter, your family and your lives, will return to a sense of normalcy.

Prayer for Joy

Father God, in the name of Jesus we come before you in humble submission. We come before the Throne of Grace, because we, your daughters, stand in need, and you said, "Come to me," Father, you said, "Seek, Me," Father, you said, "Healing is the Children's bread." Father, we ask right now for healing of our minds. Jesus, you were bruised for our iniquities, the chastisement of our peace was upon you, and by your stripes we are healed. Healed in our hearts, healed in our minds, healed in our emotions. Healed everywhere there has been a breach. Father, cause us to hear laughter again, cause us to smile again, cause us to rejoice again. This is our prayer, in Jesus's name. Amen.

12. An Emotionally Abused, Weary Mother

Thou hast turned for me my mourning into dancing: Thou hast put off my sackcloth, and girded me with gladness Psalm 30:11 (KJV)

I believe this description fit me to a T. I had so many, too many, irons in the fire. I was a mother and a daughter and a wife. I was trying to be all things to all people, and I was not doing a very good job at any of it.

So rather than being truly in control of my own life, I was too busy, I was too distracted to see what was happening in my home. I left myself open emotionally to be abused by a man who was a predator. He was a hunter in the very real sense of the word.

Jack would go up north, or at least that's what he said he was doing. He would describe his trips to me when he returned, and I can only assume he was telling the truth. At that point in time I trusted him. I didn't know. How could I know?

He would tell me all about it—how he would sit in the "blinds" for hours, waiting and watching for deer. He described how he would wait for the opportune time to strike, patiently watching for the target to enter the strike zone, luring the target in with pieces of meat or whatever other lure he had.

Later, I came to understand the importance of these hunts. I came to understand that luring in his prey was part of his game. It was part of the manipulation. It's what he did to Nikki. It's what he did to how many others? At the time, however, I was far too distracted; I was far too busy doing everything I *thought* was the right thing to do to notice that so much of what was going on was *not* right at all.

Jack was a fisherman as well. He had tons and tons of fishing poles and lures. He spent so much time cultivating his hobby. He made his own weights to sink the lures down into the water. He took pride in knowing exactly how to catch whatever prey he had in his sights. Then there were the boats for fishing and the dogs for hunting. He had all that he needed to ensnare his victims. He talked about the different types of wild game: pigs, frogs, and coon. He talked about how it felt to pursue his game, how he enjoyed tracking and trapping and, ultimately, controlling his quarry. I listened to it all. I listened with all the interest a weary, emotionally drained wife could muster; and all the while, I didn't realize he had my daughter in his crosshairs!

Prayer for Dancing

Heavenly Father, we come before you now thanking you, O God that you and you alone can turn sorrow into laughter, heartache into rejoicing, and return unto us the joy of our salvation. Lord, you and you alone can take these, your mothers, and turn their mourning into dancing. Father, cause them to know the joy of the Lord is their strength.

Cause them to see the good in difficult situations, Father, cause them to let you shape this situation, and even in this you can be exalted. This is our prayer for your mothers today, Father, as difficult, as impossible as it may seem for them at this moment, let their spirit leap and know that they shall dance again. In Jesus's name we pray. Amen.

13. My Friend Zoloft

Weeping may endure for a night, but joy cometh in the morning.
Psalm 30:5 (KJV)

What is it like to have your heart ripped out of your body? To have it handed to you to look at? That's how I felt. My heart had just been torn apart from me. It was no longer attached to my body.

I still looked the same. I still walked, talked, cooked and cleaned. I continued to do what I needed to do. I dropped the kids off at their activities. But something on the inside had changed, *drastically*.

I felt as though I'd become completely empty. There was nothing on the inside. I was now merely a hollow shell. That's the best description I have to explain what was going on within me. At the same time, though, my thoughts raced. I had a hundred mental images, visuals in my head that I couldn't bear to see. Yet they erupted in my mind over and over and over again.

The reality of my life was what it was. My daughter had been abused. There was nothing I could do to turn back the clock. There was nothing I could do to undo the unspeakable horror that had been done.

Yet, in my mind, I was trying to catch Jack in the act of molesting my daughter. If I could only catch him, I thought, I could stop it. I could somehow change the reality that I knew could not be changed. A variety of different, imagined scenes continued to replay in my mind and, just as we do when we watch a video on television, I thought I could rewind. I wanted to rewind to the last segment, the one we'd just seen, the one that needed to be changed.

But this was real life, and although I knew this in my head, I continued to try to catch him. If only I could catch him, I could make him stop. If only I could catch him, I could erase all that had happened, just as you might erase a mistake on paper.

I began living in my own private dream world. I absolutely knew that somehow, I was going to make what was wrong right. I absolutely knew there had to be a way to have a "do-over." I knew we could somehow do this all differently. There had to be a way to change the ending and make the awfulness for my daughter go away.

Although I tried with all my might, I realized I could not change the ending for her. I could not change the ending for me. I could not turn back the hands of time and make it different. I couldn't un-marry Jack Reiss. I had married a sick, disgusting human being who had abused my little girl, and I could not change that. All of these thoughts were taking their toll.

Throughout this time, neither Nikki nor I could sleep. We were a mess. Neither one of us could focus on anything more than the very simplest of tasks. I knew we needed to get some help. I knew we needed to calm down and maybe even get some sleep. So we made a visit to our family doctor, who gave us each a prescription for Zoloft.

I have to say that I am not a fan of anti-depressants. I personally believe there are too many side effects and that it is too easy to get hooked. However, under certain circumstances and for a period of time, I had no problem with anti-anxiety medicines that can help a person "get over the hump." I knew that such a circumstance was before me. Now was that period of time.

With much caution after a previous, and especially harrowing experience I'd had with my daughter, I accepted that we needed this prescription. I knew we needed the help, but I also knew I had to carefully control what Nikki had access to.

The experience that made me so hesitant to have Zoloft in the house happened shortly after Nikki had disclosed to me, and the news of her abuse was starting to wash across our small town. I had come home from bible study and found Nikki in our dining room. She was sitting by the roll-top desk with a bottle of pills spilled all around her.

"What are you doing?" I asked with alarm.

She looked at me sadly. I will never forget how calmly she told me that the only reason she didn't take those pills was that my mother, her grandmother, would not be able to handle it.

My heart broke yet again. The only reason my precious baby girl did not kill herself—her only reason for not committing suicide that night in an attempt to stop her pain—was the love she had for her grandmother.

I grabbed those pills away from her, and I never gave them back. I remember thinking, "Thank you, God!"

There sat my sweet, innocent daughter again, putting her concern for everyone else ahead of any concern for herself. Just as she had done when she stayed silent about her abuse to protect me from the fact that she was being molested by my husband. She put her grandmother before herself, and this time she was right. I thank God for that, this time it saved her life.

This time around, however, when we couldn't sleep and we couldn't focus and we needed the pills to help us get over the hump, I hid the meds. I hid them so well that there was a point in time when even I couldn't find them. Nikki was not very happy with me.

Over time, we learned to sleep without the pills. I refilled those bottles a couple of times, but eventually we let them go. We never finished the prescription.

Prayer for Protection

Father God, in the name of your son, Jesus, we come before you asking you to protect our daughters from self-harming behaviors. Lord, they are still young and not as able to cope with the trauma. Father, they do not understand they have an enemy that plays for keeps. Our enemy, Satan, wants to take our children out while they are young, thereby rendering them ineffective to do your work and fulfill your purposes and plans for them on this earth.

Father, we come against that now in the name of Jesus; we cancel every attack on our daughter's life, her mind, her emotions, we say right now that she will blossom, she will be healed, she will be restored, fulfilled, protected, covered, and know that she is loved and cared for in the name of Jesus. Amen.

14. The Must-Have Discussion

Therefore we do not lose heart. Though outwardly we are wasting away, yet inwardly we are being renewed day by day. [17] For our light and momentary troubles are achieving for us an eternal glory that far outweighs them all. [18] So we fix our eyes not on what is seen, but on what is unseen, since what is seen is temporary, but what is unseen is eternal. 2 Corinthians 4:16-18 (NIV)

I must remind you again this book is written to and for the mothers of sexually abused children. This section is *not* "G" rated. Neither is it rated "X." In fact, it simply isn't rated because there's no way to do so. It is a discussion that must be had. It isn't easy. It isn't pleasant. It is painful and sometimes brutally honest. It isn't a discussion that you will soon forget.

This *is* a discussion that will be more difficult for some than for others. Yet it is a conversation that you MUST have, and you must have it sooner rather than later. The sooner you talk about this with your daughter, the sooner she can begin mentally to process what happened to her.

My daughter was a teenager when she disclosed to me what had happened to her since she was only seven or eight years old.

She was fifteen years old when she told me. She was busty, petite, and as cute as a button. She had some physical ailments such as hay fever, allergies and psoriasis, all which were constant and reoccurring throughout her childhood. Because she had struggled with these illnesses, she had already dealt with anxiety.

Nikki disclosed her story to me at night. The very next day when she came home from school, I remember being in the garage with her. We were in the car where we could talk in private, and I reiterated, "Nikki, this is not your fault. You bear no responsibility. This is 100 percent *his* fault. Abuse is the adult's shortcomings, the adult's doings."

She gave me a look that said, "Sure Mom, whatever you say…but you don't know the whole story."

Again I stress that this is why you *must* have this discussion immediately after disclosure.

"Nikki," I told my daughter, "the fact that your body had a physical response to the repetition of the act is completely and naturally normal. That is the way God made us. That has nothing to do with a forty-plus-year-old man sexually molesting an innocent little girl, which is what you were. You are getting confused with who you are now and who you were when he began grooming you for the abuse. You are *not to blame.*"

As she turned her face away to look down, I took my hand and gently lifted her head and said to her, "Look at me. Look me dead in the eye. Just because your body has a physical reaction does not, *does not,* mean you played any part in this. It *does not mean that you were a willing participant.* You, my dear daughter, were a victim of a sick, sick man, and you have nothing to be ashamed of. You hold your head up high."

Mothers, it is so very important to talk to your daughters about the sexual molestation. Now is not the time to be coy. It is not the time to skip over the most obvious topic of all. Sexual molestation means there was something sexual.

TALK ABOUT IT. Don't shy away from it. Tell your daughter that yes, you know she was forced, manipulated, cajoled, and enticed into doing things she did not want to do. Tell her how sorry you are that she has had to endure this. Tell her that you are here now, and you both can talk about it when and if she wants to. Tell her, depending on her age, that without any shame she can be candid and that you can talk about what she will need to watch out for in the future. Tell her all of this—for her and for yourself.

I really do believe having this little but important discussion with Nikki early made a difference for her. She knew Mom wasn't being a prude and pretending there was no sex. It is such a difficult topic for some mothers to approach. Some mothers gloss over this vital aspect of the child's recovery, or they try to leave it to the experts.

I personally think it will do your child wonders to hear this from you. It is important for your child to hear you say it. She needs to know that *you* know there is no shame for her to carry, even with the sexual acts that were done to her and even if they occurred over a period of time. She needs to hear you say that she was not the initiator, she was not the adult, and she was not the authority figure. You must tell her she bears *no* responsibility in this at all. And she needs to hear you tell her she has your complete and total respect as a person, as an individual. Tell her she has your unwavering love. Tell her she was groomed to do what she did and she no longer has to carry that weight with her. Tell her she is released from her pain, her guilt and her shame.

Whatever you do, talk to her. Be there for her to talk to you. Even if she doesn't want to talk.

One day after the entire town knew, after everyone in the community had heard about the horror my daughter had suffered, I went into Nikki's room. She was in the closet in her bedroom with the door closed. She was crouched down, sitting with her knees pulled into her chest, both arms wrapped around her as she sat quietly and alone in the dark.

I came into the room and found her there, scrunched and hiding in a two-foot by three-foot closet. I asked her what she was doing. I pleaded that she come out of the closet and talk to me. She would not. I tried to open the closet door, but she grabbed ahold of it, trying to close herself in even more. But I would not let her. I looked at her in there, and my heart broke once again. She would not come out, and I could not fit in there with her. So I sat down outside the closet.

I told her that I was *not* going to leave until she came out. Very quietly, in the tiniest little of voices, she said to me,

"No, Mom. Just leave."

My heart broke again. But leaving her there was something I could not, would not do. There was no way I was going to leave my daughter in that closet—alone, lonely and scared. It was so obvious what she wanted. She wanted to shrink up. She wanted to disappear. But I knew that this moment was a critical point. I knew that Nikki needed to know that she was not alone, that I would just *be* with her.

I sat down outside that closet door, as close to my daughter as I could be. I didn't try to talk. I was just there. I stayed until she finally decided to come out on her own.

If you are a parent that is not comfortable with your own sexuality and you cannot see yourself having this conversation with your daughter, then just be there for her. And then have the conversation with your daughter in the presence of a professional. The most important thing is to have it as soon after the disclosure as possible so your daughter is not left to wonder, "What does my mom think of me now?"

The shame, the fear, the guilt: those who have survived being sexually abused as a child must endure them all. The molesters, and sometimes even those who should know better but don't, say whatever they can to convince a child that the abuse is his or her fault. "You are too cute," they say. "You are too sexy." "*You* make me feel this way."

These predators also commonly threaten or even bribe children, making sure that they do not speak out. They convince them they will not be believed. "I am an adult," they say. "You, after all, are just a kid. Who will believe you?"

So what does this abuse—this shame and fear and guilt—do to a child? It creates a *horror* that may never go away. Many children of abuse grow up to have extremely low self-esteem. Some end up hating themselves. They experience depression, sometimes so extreme they want to end their pain through suicide.

These faultless victims also suffer from any or all of the following:

1. Inability to Trust: Because these victims were betrayed by those they loved and trusted, they learn that they can no longer trust.

2. Difficulty with Sexual Intimacy: When children who have been abused reach adulthood, many struggle with becoming intimate sexually. Their first experiences with sex were abusive. Their painful, shame-ridden memories can rise up and make any intimate pleasure impossible.

3. Inability to Sleep: Those who've endured sexual abuse can have something similar to post-traumatic stress disorder. The resulting anxiety can make it difficult to sleep.

4. Dissociation: Children of abuse can become disconnected — from their own brain functions. As they endured the unendurable, their minds may have learned to refuse to connect with the feelings, thoughts, and memories. In extreme cases, children develop dissociated personalities, which affects their sense of identity.

5. Reliving the Abuse: Some victims of abuse find themselves regularly reliving the sexual encounters as though it is happening in the present.

6. Repeat Victimization: Studies have shown that survivors of sexual abuse may end up in another abusive relationship. Female rape victims under eighteen are two times more likely to be raped as an adult. Additionally, as these young

victims of sexual abuse grow into adulthood, many develop specific means of coping in an effort to ward off the feelings of fear and loss of power they lived with when they were young.

7. Grief: Survivors of childhood abuse often grieve for the childhood they never had. The years they should have been spending as a happy, innocent child were stolen from them by their abuser. They mourn the loss of fun and innocence they never had.

8. Food Abuse: Those who were sexually abused as children may lose all control or take obsessive control of their eating habits. They do so for two reasons: as an attempt to find a way to deny any responsibility for the abuse, or as a way to forcefully take back the control that they lost.

9. Substance Abuse: Many survivors find that alcohol and/or prescription or illegal drugs can help them run from the power of their memories and their inability to cope with their feelings.

10. Self-mutilation: Harming oneself is another tragic way children of sexual abuse try to cope. Cutting and burning are two common methods of inflicting pain upon themselves these now-adults use to overcome the pain of abuse.

I *cannot* stress to you enough how important it is to talk to your daughter. Many survivors of child abuse do not tell anyone as they suffer through something so horrible that no child should *ever* be expected to suffer through. You must have the discussion. You must talk.

You must sit outside the closet door as your daughter curls herself within. You must patiently wait and then somehow find a way to let her talk. You must sit there and wait until she comes out on her own. You must.

Prayer for Courage and Compassion

Heavenly Father, we come before you now with these, your mothers, on behalf of their daughters. Father, we ask for your guardian angels to protect these your daughters, Father. Lord, we pray that no hurt, harm, nor danger would come near to them. We pray now for your wisdom in this situation, your wisdom in this circumstance, your wisdom in this dilemma.

Father, we are not sure which way to go, and Father, too many missteps have already been made. We don't want to take another step without hearing from you, God. Father, speak to us now, speak clearly so that we know beyond a shadow of a doubt we are following your leading and guidance Father. Your word says my sheep hear my voice and another they will not follow. Lord, give us the courage to go forward in the direction you give, come what may.

This is our prayer in Jesus's name. Amen.

15. God's Going to Get the Glory

That the trial of your faith, being much more precious than of gold that perisheth, though it be tried with fire, might be found unto praise and honour and glory at the appearing of Jesus Christ: 1 Peter 1:7 (KJV)

For the first couple of days after Nikki disclosed what had happened, I kept looking at her and saying "God's going to get some glory out of this!" She would look at me with bewilderment. One day she finally asked, "What does that mean?"

When she asked me what I meant by saying that, I wasn't sure how to explain it. I really didn't have the words for her at the time. It was so brand new. The information was new, and I didn't know what to think about any of it. I was still processing what had taken place. But I knew in my spirit, way down deep to my very core, that if God had allowed something this horrific to happen to my daughter that in the end, His name would be exalted.

I knew He would not have allowed something so horrible to happen, were it not somehow going to bring Him glory.

I didn't know how, I didn't know when, but I did know.

Romans 8:28; the words resonate throughout my spirit: "The passage doesn't tell us that all things are good. Rather, it says all things work or will work together, ultimately, for the good. This is and has been my saying."

Everything we go through in life, obviously, is not always good. Some things are painful. Some things are detrimental. Some things leave us wondering why this thing, whatever *this thing* might be, has happened. We wonder how and, most importantly, why this thing could happen to us.

From the very beginning, I believed with everything in my heart that somehow, some way, when this incident was considered or mentioned in the future, when it was brought up in any context, the faithfulness of the Lord would be an intricate thread woven throughout the account. I didn't understand exactly why I thought that. I simply did. I knew without a doubt that God would be honored. I understand now that that is what I meant when I told my daughter that God would get some glory out of this.

Today I can tell you that this has proven to be true.

So many people witnessed the Lord working in our lives as we endured all we had to endure. Those who were with us throughout the criminal proceedings observed the way we-Nikki, myself and my entire family- handled ourselves. People saw our commitment to each other, and they saw our strength. They saw our trust in God. They watched the way we conducted ourselves, and they commented on the strength and power of our faith. Watching us stand firmly in our faith and our love ultimately brought them closer to Him. It gave them strength, peace, and faith in their own personal walks with the Lord. God got some glory out of this!

Prayer for Faith

Father God, in the name of Jesus we come before you, because you are good, because your kind, because you are all-knowing and all-loving that we thank you, God. We bring these your daughters, mothers, sisters before you, God. Thank you, God, that you give strength, you give them the fortitude, you give them everything that they need.

You said that without faith it is impossible to please you. So that even while you are trying our faith right now that even though you try us, you still give us what we need to get through it. In order to get through the test, O God, even through the tears, even through the heartache, even through the pain, and the hurt. I ask that you cause your daughters to know that you are with them even through the pain.

You said you'd never leave us or forsake but that you would be with us always and forever, even to the end of the world. I pray that your women will seek your face as never before; in this we pray in Jesus's name. Amen.

16. Church Meeting

The steadfast love of the Lord never ceases; his mercies never come to an end; they are new every morning; great is your faithfulness. Lamentations 3:22-23 (KJV)

Jack and I first met at the church I'd been attending since I'd returned to Michigan in the summer of 1996. I'd attended this very same church, and had been baptized there as a child. After leaving my first husband, Nikki and Jordan's father, in Maryland, I returned to the church I knew; the church that was a part of my home. It just so happened that Jack was the organist there. He was married and had two adolescent children.

I began dating Jack in early 1999, after his wife had left him and moved to another state. He was separated, but not divorced. He moved into my home with me and my children in September, 1999, and we became a family. We were married in May of 2000. He loved my children (or so I thought).

Initially, he was a fun and a kind person. He was the kind of man you could always count on, offering assistance to anyone who needed it. When it came to vehicles, small engines, and home repairs, he was a Jack of all trades. The man could fix anything.

Jack didn't work. He was disabled from a motorcycle accident that occurred earlier in his life. He had broken his right leg so badly that he had two plates and seventeen rods in place holding it together. Yet he was able to do nearly anything he really wanted to do. He hunted, fished, golfed, camped, and boated. He swam and danced; and he drank.

Even though he was disabled by definition, he did so much. By the time our marriage ended, I can remember telling him to get a job. After all, he could do anything he wanted to do!

During our marriage we did a fair amount of traveling, journeying to different parts of the country. We visited with his family at their reunions in August of every year. We went to San Francisco, Arkansas, Tennessee, Mackinaw Island, Chicago, Portland, and Maryland. He enjoyed driving, and I enjoyed being right there next to him in the passenger seat.

I enjoyed being married. I enjoyed the children having a male presence in their life. Because Nikki and Jordan's father lived halfway across the country in Maryland and because his new wife made their relationship difficult to sustain, the kids weren't able to see their dad as much as they liked. I was happy and secure in the idea that Jack could give my children the male role model they needed.

The fairy tale didn't last though, and the marriage began to unravel fairly quickly. I had a demanding job, and Jack, in my opinion, did a whole lot of nothing. The Bible calls this being "unequally yoked." Most people translate that into the idea of not being on the same level. In this case, both were absolutely true.

I was educated and on the move. I was determined and a go-getter. Jack was not. As our time together continued, I began to travel down a different spiritual path than him. I chose to stop doing many of the things that in the beginning we had enjoyed doing together. I stopped drinking and going to clubs with him. I stopped playing cards. I began to seek a deeper relationship with God. The changes I was making became a point of contention in our marriage. He did not at all like who I was becoming. I was not sure I liked who he was either.

It wasn't too much longer until I knew for sure that I did not at all like the person I was married to. Jack began to watch pornography around me. He became addicted. A friend of his showed him a way to access porn inexpensively, and he began to watch it all the time. He would spend his entire days watching. He wanted me to watch with him, and one time I did. I knew immediately that it was not something I could continue to be involved in. I didn't like it, and I didn't understand his attraction.

That became another point of contention between us. I couldn't understand: Why did he need to watch it all the time? What exactly did it say about him? Here was the church organist continually feeding his mind with pornography. He watched early in the morning. He would be watching in the middle of the day when I came home from work. He watched late at night after we'd all gone to bed. He became obsessed. He tore off the covers and the labels and brought video tapes into our home. Jordan told me later, after Jack and I had divorced, that he saw one of the videos in passing.

It got to the point that Jack had discs in his car. He actually set up a DVD player in his car, in the front, by the radio so he could have access to his porn each and every time he got behind the wheel. He had pornography ready and accessible anytime and anywhere he wanted it.

During this time, I would walk into the room and he would turn the television completely off. It was apparent what he was doing. I became thoroughly repulsed with him as a human begin. I lost any respect for him I might have once had, and I began to distrust him. You know the old saying, "Where there's smoke, there's fire"? I found both!

As my suspicions grew, they began to be confirmed. I found condoms in his vehicle and among his personal things. He tried to tell me the condoms were old, that they'd been there a long time that they were from his past. Time and time again, he reassured me he was being faithful. But I'd been here before, and I knew what it felt like. I had lived in this state of distrust and suspicion when I was married to my first husband. I knew exactly what I was dealing with.

Jack had a dark side. He was manipulative and controlling. He was verbally abusive. He wouldn't lie to me so much as he would omit things. He told half-truths. He was evasive and vague, and he would be ambiguous with facts. He would leave the house and not come home for two or three days at a time. But he always had a reason, actually an excuse, for everything. He was a martyr of his own making, in his own mind.

I finally wised up. I found my courage and strength, and I filed for separation. At that point, once I'd finally reached the end of my patience with him, he began to understand. He finally got it that I was on my way out. He began to apologize. He asked for another chance, which was very hard for me to deny. I thought about staying. After all, I reasoned, I had already divorced once. Because God doesn't like divorce, I thought about staying and trying to make it work. But, ultimately, I knew I couldn't stay.

Jack was who he was. Of course he tried to paint over his stripes. He desperately tried to convince me that he wasn't the man I thought he was. But he was. He continued to make mistakes, proving that he was truly the beast I'd begin to think he was.

So I began to pray. I prayed fervently.

I will never forget the day I was downstairs by the washing machine and from somewhere within me I heard the word "reprobate."

I spoke back, "Oh God," I asked, "Is this what I'm dealing with?"

Does he have a reprobate mind? I could not believe what I'd heard, and yet I could. I knew this man. I knew what he was. I knew, indeed.

"Well, God," I continued, "if you've given up on him, surely I don't have to stay married to him." I remembered this Bible verse:

"And even as they did not like to retain God in their knowledge, God gave them over to a reprobate mind, to do those things which are not convenient;" Romans 1:28 (KJV)

I knew that God was telling me that this man I found myself married to was morally depraved. I knew I had been given my marching orders. That was my "okay" from the Lord, telling me that it was all right, in fact, that it was necessary, to divorce this man. From that moment on, I did not turn back.

A Prayer for New Mercies

Dear Father, we your daughters, mothers, children of the Most High God, come before you, our Father, broken, hurt, lonely, betrayed, rejected, ashamed, distrustful, scared, and in sheer shock of what has taken place with our children. Father, this is the most difficult thing that has happened to us in our entire life. We want to turn back the hands of time so that this never took place; we want to change some of our choices so that our children are safe, but, Lord, we can't.

So, Father God, we come to you asking for the new mercies your word says we can have, and your faithfulness. Lord, we are asking that you hold our hands as we face a brand new day. You said you wouldn't leave us nor forsake us…we are holding on to that promise with every fiber of our being. In Jesus's name we pray. Amen.

17. Hindsight's 20/20

I acknowledged my sin to you and did not cover up my iniquity, I said, "I will confess my transgressions to the Lord, and you forgave the guilt of my sin. Psalms 32:5

Jack came from a large family. He was the only boy out of four children. Although his father was deceased he, his mother, sisters and their children were very close. They were the kind of family so many in the rest of the world aspire to be. They regularly came together to have Sunday dinners; and enjoyed being together as a family.

These were, for all appearances, good people. Throughout the years, Jack's mother had lovingly opened her home to children who had no home of their own. She was a loving, giving woman who had been a foster parent for many years. Many of the children she brought into her home were special needs children. She even adopted a few of the children she had fostered. As far as anyone could tell, they were a good and prayerful family. Sitting around their table before meals, I loved that we would reach out and take one another's hands. We would ask God for His blessings and His grace.

I liked Jack's family. They were kind to me and to my children. They accepted us and brought us easily into their fold. For the most part, Nikki and Jordan liked being around the other kids that Jack's mom was raising at the time. My eldest son Jared, however, had a few reservations. He wasn't always as comfortable as his siblings had been with his new family. He had never liked Jack. "He's not what he pretends to be, Mom," he would tell me. When I finally had the courage to tell Jared about Nikki's molestation, he was furious. He'd known that something wasn't right, and I hadn't listened.

71

As we grew together as a family, Jack and I enjoyed our early years together. We would go out to dinner and to the movies. We drank socially, and we both liked to dance. We had a lot of fun together. He was always so nice. He was nice to me and to my children. He was nice to my mom and to my dad. He was nice to my brothers and to my extended family. In the beginning, he was, or at least he appeared to be, simply a very nice and very decent man. Together the two of us eventually became foster parents ourselves, and we always included our foster kids in what we did.

Because I'd been a single mom, my mother sometimes watched my children. When I married Jack, however, he insisted that I no longer allow her to do so. He insisted that now that we were a couple, the children should be with him. He would say to me, "Lisa, I'm here now. Let those kids come home. I know I'm not their father, but I'm here now. *I'm your help.*" He said this to me over and over again. Now I know why he was so anxious to be a father figure to my children. Now I know why it was so important for him to have my children in the home while I was at work.

Mothers in our desperation to have a father figure for our children, please I be you, don't make the same mistake I did. Don't offer your children up to be devoured by the evil that's lurking waiting, watching for whom it may devour. Our children are too precious.

I was so grateful to him for that. It isn't easy to be a single mom. It isn't easy to raise two young children alone. A mom needs help; and here was this nice, decent, caring, and God-fearing man who loved me and wanted to be my help. That's what I thought. Maybe that's what I wanted to think. It's so evident now that he had an ulterior motive. It's beyond obvious that he manipulated me at every single turn. I know because that's what molesters do. I know who he is and what he did. I can honestly say I doubt that he ever really loved me.

Jordan was in kindergarten, Nikki in the third grade. Jack went fishing a lot and would always take the two youngest kids with him.

He took Nikki and Jordan, but I later found out that he would send Jordan off somewhere and he would molest Nikki. Nikki told me that Jack would say to her, if she did "whatever" to him, she could stay home from school that day.

Jack was the ultimate hunter, and he had stalked his prey. He used pretenses and facades. He craftily wore a mask to conceal who he really was and what he really wanted. Now I know why it was so important for him to *help* me with the kids. I know why he continued to argue and even berate me when I asked my mother to watch them. He wanted Nikki close and available. He wanted my daughter nearby, because he wanted to abuse her.

Later in our marriage, when we were already having trouble, Jack and I went to a couple's event for Valentine's Day. Near the end of the event we were instructed to write a love letter to our spouse. Because there was a bit of time left, some of the participants were able to read to the group the letters they had written. Jack volunteered to read out loud to the group his love letter to me. I was touched by what seemed, at the time, to be his love for me. I was anxious to hear what he had to say. He didn't get a chance to read what he had written, though, as the time ran out.

When we got home that Valentine's Day evening, he went to his corner, as was our typical behavior at this point in our marriage, and I went to mine and that was the end of that. He never mentioned the letter again, and neither did I. He never gave me the letter.

Although I didn't want to admit it, because I wanted to be loved, I knew he had not been sincere in expressing his love in that letter. "This is all about the show," I remember thinking. "There's nothing real at all. He simply wanted to read me this love letter in front of other people. He just wanted to *appear* to love me." This was simply another attempt to make himself look good; to make others think he was something other than what he really was.

Jack would often take the children with him to the store. He would take them fishing or out to see his mom. Just as he needed to appear to care for me, he needed to appear to care for my children. Having them with him was never a problem for him. At the time I saw this as a good thing. He loves my kids, I thought. He's willing to put his own needs aside to help me care for my children.

How stupid can one person be? All child molesters want to be around children. They are the coaches, teachers, and volunteers. They are the clergy and the Boy and Girl Scout leaders. They befriend the children, and they befriend the parents. You cannot be too careful nowadays. I now see everyone as a suspect. When it comes to keeping children safe, I have no trust. I am jaded.

I know everyone is not a molester, yet I am forever on the lookout. I am in a perpetual state of high alert, as I have never been before and I feel that I am not wrong. I am not ashamed of my doubts. A good healthy dose of suspicion for any parent would serve our children well in a country where this scourge is running rampant. A good healthy dose of suspicion is needed in a country in which its babies are being molested. It is an insidious epidemic that must be checked.

While initially Jack's family accepted me and welcomed me into his family as his wife, that welcome did not last. Once he was indicted, I became the Wicked Witch of the West as far as his family was concerned. "You put Nikki up to this!" they cried. They said so many hateful things to me and even more hateful things about me. Eventually his family stopped speaking to me. For his family, I ceased to exist.

I was also harassed by the adolescents in his family, by his adopted sisters and his nieces, who would call me in the middle of the night and hang up the phone. Or they would call and say something inane such as, "Is Jack there?" I could hear the girls in the background giggling. I know that it was just stupid kids pulling stupid pranks, but it made it very clear to me what was being said in their homes. It became obvious the types of things the adults were saying around the children. What the adults were saying somehow gave the children permission to harass me.

It seemed that, at least to his family, I was the problem. The problem was not the fact that my daughter had been molested all these years by their family member. No, Instead of feeling any anger toward Jack, his family decided it was time to "lock and load" to defeat their perceived enemy, that villain being me. After all, they concluded, I had put Nikki up to this; I had choreographed the entire drama. I finally had a trace put on my phone, but I was determined not to change my number. I was not going to let them make me lose complete control of my life.

I truly have no idea what Jack told his family and whether or not they actually believed him. Part of me believes they knew the truth. Another part of me says that he was a grown man who had lived his entire life away from them. He had not lived with them for years. Perhaps they truly did not know. But then I would wince as I began to think about all the foster children his mother had cared for. I would think about all those children he'd had access to.

I believed in my heart of hearts that he MUST HAVE done this to someone else. He must have gone after another innocent little child. Certainly, I decided, they had been covering up for this man all this time. I knew they would unite as a family to protect their own; that they would chastise anyone who spoke out against him. I knew they would never allow a foster child to say anything to malign their "Jacky". No. I knew they would not.

It became quite clear to me that Jack's family thought he could do no wrong. If any child dared to speak of this unthinkable act done by *their* Jack, the child would certainly receive a "beheading" of sorts. With absolutely no doubt whatsoever, I am sure the children whom he molested quietly endured until they could get away.

After the trial I talked with others who, throughout the years, had heard of what Jack had done. They were out there, and they had known. Or at least they had heard and they had suspected. They did not speak out at the trial because they, very simply, had been hushed by his family. To this day, even as I write these words, people come to me and tell me of the atrocities that Jack perpetuated on the innocent and often, the mentally challenged in our community.

It's a terrible thing that so many people suspected Jack and yet nothing was ever done. He had gotten away with all of it or so many years.

I simply will never believe that a forty-year-old man looked at my Nikki and "suddenly" decided he would begin molesting children. According to the evidence currently available, that is simply not the way molestation happens. Anyone who works with these predators, with adult male child molesters- not with an adolescent molesting a younger child or with children experimenting with sex- but with an adult man who targets and grooms an eight-year-old child, will tell you this has happened before. They will tell you that this has definitely happened before, over and over and over again.

Prayer of Repentance

Father God, we come before you asking that you clean us up where we misstep and go astray. We ask, Father, that you purify us, your daughters, that you make us every whit whole. We ask right now for your purifying fire to come in, clean up every area of our life, our heart, our body, our mind, O God, that's not like you. We ask right now, as it's you and you alone, we have sinned before. You can come in with that refiner's fire as we acknowledge our sin and turn from it.

We stand before you, God, we repent before you, our maker and our creator, our God, our Father, and the Holy One of Israel. We ask for your forgiveness, and we accept it without fear, without shame, and without condemnation. Dear Father, you said that if we would do that, you would remove the sin from us as far as the east is from the west. In Jesus's name we walk away with our heads held high, no longer bound to what we were, did, or didn't do. In Jesus's name we pray. Amen.

18. Seeing the Devil First-hand

For we wrestle not against flesh and blood, but against principalities, against powers, against the rulers of darkness of this world, against spiritual wickedness in high places. Ephesians 6:12 (KJV)

When you recognize evil, when you come to understand this horrific incident in the way that I did, it will be time to say, in the way that I did, "I have lost enough." It is at that point that you mustn't let the enemy gain another step. You must fight to take back everything that was stolen, to dig in your heels, to set your face like a flint and to get into position. You must fight like hell! You must get down on your knees and fight for yourself and for your daughter. You must refuse to let the enemy win.

Yes. The devil has won a skirmish. Yes, he has won a huge battle. But you must say to yourself, "I'll be doggone if he is going to win this war!" You must fight to make sure that his is not the total destruction of you, nor of your daughter, nor or your family. You must be determined that the suffering ends and the healing begins.

This is exactly how I've survived the horror. I determined that I would fight. I determined I would turn to a God that would help me fight. I turned to the fact that if my precious daughter, my baby, could deal with this, then I could hang in there and fight for her. I knew that I would fight until the end. I knew that nothing and nobody would defeat us.

You may, as I did, come to the point of rage, and that's okay. In fact, I believe it is one of the healthiest things you can do. Rather than lying down in that darkness and wallowing in the unbearable pain, you must embrace that rage. You can say it: "Devil, you have made me mad now!" God has given us words to fight with.

Matthew 11:12 (KJV) says, "...the kingdom of heaven suffers violence, and the violent take it by force." It is time for you to take the violence that has been suffered upon your daughter, upon you and your entire family, by force. It is time to get mad and to fight back!

You can know that God is there to help you in your fight against this unspeakable evil. The Lord promises us in 2 Corinthians that He is with us in our struggle and in our pain, and we can be strong:

"For the weapons of our warfare are not carnal, but mighty through God to the pulling down of strong holds" (10:4) KJV

He promises that our victory can be mighty through Him. He promises us hope, but I'm telling you to *expect* another attack. Do not be caught off guard. We are not ignorant of his tactics and his schemes, as he is forever trying to trip us up. We must see him coming. We must know that it is him, rearing his ugly little head, and we must cut him off at the pass.

Do not give in! Do not give up!

Understand that the devil is doing what he has always done. Know that he does not fight fair. When he thinks he has you down, when he thinks you have no strength left to fight that is when he will go for the jugular. You must be prepared. You must remain prayerful. Do not, I repeat, do not throw up your hand in despair. Giving up is what he wants you to do. So you must fight. You must fight for yourself and for your sanity. You must fight for your peace, for your future, for your daughter and for your family. You must fight for your life. You must fight because you and all those whom you love deserve it.

Prayer for Strategic Weapons

Father God, we come before you right now and, God, hear this our prayer, our petition, and our plea. Father, you know what we are battling with right now, and you know how the enemy has come after us. But God, we plead the blood of Jesus and say this far and no farther! God, we come against that enemy right now and we say we have taken a stand, a foothold, and we shall not be moved!

Father speak to us as you did David; give us the plan and the strategy to combat this enemy as we know that the ultimate victory will belong to you! Father, we seek you, we will pray, we will fast, we will plead the blood over our children. Lord, we wait for you to show us the plans of the enemy. We are like Habakkuk, Father, we will sit and wait to see what you will say to us. In Jesus's name we pray. Amen.

19. A Violation of Trust

And ye shall know the truth, and the truth shall make you free   John 8:32 (KJV)

Where does a mother go for support, to be heard, to be understood, to get help for her child when that child has been abused? She has to have a place to fall apart, and yet she must be strong to give her child the support her child needs.

Because I had already divorced this man who abused my precious daughter, there were no conflicting feelings; there was no pull, no tug of heart strings still left. There was no love lost.

I had Jack out of my house and I knew that although a horror had taken place, my daughter was now safe. What about those mothers and wives who are in a different situation? What about the mothers and wives who remain in the home with the abuser? What can they do? How can they be safe? I know beyond a shadow of a doubt that first we must protect our daughters and our sons.

Yet because of the research I have done, and because of the case studies I have read, I now know that so many of you thought you had taken steps to do something to protect your child. Sadly, the steps were far too inadequate. Because you trusted this perpetrator, the results have been devastating.

Equally devastating is that, some of you unsuspecting mothers allowed the perpetrator back into your home, allowing the molestation to begin again.

Our children deserve so much more. Our children are the ones who deserve our trust. That person manipulating and lying to you, that perpetrator most certainly does not deserve your trust. That rascal deserves only your distrust. It is your responsibility to expect the molestation to continue, not to hope it won't.

You must do what must be done. You must stand up for your child. In the news of late, reports of incest involving children from the Duggar Family, stars of a popular reality television show '*19 and Counting.*' This scourge of molestation happened in their home, amongst with their own biological children, yet they did not initially react to removing their son (who was the aggressor), and ultimately, revictimization occurred.

The steps taken were too little, although there were steps taken, if this is you, and you see yourself in this situation, please act immediately and know your daughter is counting on you. Do not expect that things will change on their own, they will not. You must expect the molestation to continue. Don't believe the lie. You must be your child's voice and show the strength for them that you have not shown before. Your child deserves this strength, and the truth of the matter is…YOU DO TOO!

You see, incest is not only a violation of the child; it is also a violation of the mother. I know this may seem strange, but I also feel completely violated. The cliché that says if you've never experienced it you probably won't understand it really does fit here. Here was this person whom I did love at one time, a person whom I trusted with the only things on this earth that I love, my children.

The goal of a child molester is to "groom" your child, to take them down a path, step by insidious step, to get the child to the ultimate goal; and in a predator's sick and twisted mind, that goal is molestation.

In the case of my daughter, Jack Reiss began grooming Nikki when she was a young child. When she was only in the second grade he began by showing her pornography, to convince her that it was okay to see these images.

I will always remember the moment that Nikki finally came to understand that she had been groomed for her abuse, that it was not her fault, that she had been only a little girl who had little choice but to trust what her stepfather was doing to her. It was during Christmas of 2006 when Nikki saw her little cousin playing sweetly in the other room. We were at the kitchen table and I said, "Nikki, that's how young you were when he began messing with you."

It was a breakthrough moment for her. She finally got it. It wasn't the fifteen-year-old Nikki that Jack Reiss began grooming. It was the sweet, innocent, little girl, that she was, that Jack Reiss began grooming, touching, messing with, perverting for his own twisted purposes. I saw the light bulb come on in her, and I also saw her get mad when she finally realized what had happened to her and the childhood that she did not have, because of this sick individual.

I praised God that she could perhaps let go of some of her guilt which she had mistakenly taken on as her own, which was misplaced, he guilt always belongs with the adult the authority figure.

We, society in general, know that the vast majority of molesters are not strangers. They are someone the child knows and trusts. They are most often a family member or a family friend. We know that they first gain the child's trust. That is how they begin to groom the child for what will come later. For example, these molesters start to play with the child more and more. They may "accidently" touch the child while they are playing. Or they may bribe the child with gifts or toys. They are very good at finding something the child likes, something they can use to get what *they* want.

As I look back, I can now see the things Jack did for Nikki. My daughter loved pickles, the big ones you get at party stores. Jack always bought her pickles. He had a "special" relationship with her, which means he favored her.

He showed her all kinds of attention, and the truth is she needed it, her father was 500 miles away and never called her. Her elder brother was 7 years older than her and found her a pest. She was an only girl and very sensitive. She was picked on for being the only girl, and as the only girl myself, I saw that and often came to her rescue.

The night prior to our marriage, Jack let Nikki give him a haircut, she was eight years old. Nikki had such fun with that, and, at the time, I thought it was sweet. Again this was another means to gain her trust which he could at a later time for his sick purposes.

After our divorce, one of his sisters commented, "I hope Lisa doesn't discourage Nikki and Jack's special relationship." Ha. Now we know what a very special relationship he had developed with my daughter. All at Nikki's expense. All to my daughter's horror. When you hear about a special relationship, your ears should peak, and the hair on your skin raised, please pay attention this could be a clue.

The gifts, the attention, the "special" times spent together- all are nothing more than a molester's ploy to gain his victim's trust. If you know or hear of an adult with a "special" relationship with a child, I urge you to look deeper into this. I urge you to do everything you can to make absolutely sure that this child is safe.

I sometimes wonder if Jack himself had been molested as a child. Maybe that is the reason he is who he is. Maybe someone he had trusted had violated him. I know this is one of the ways molesters begin. They were molested themselves and then begin to do to others what had been done to them.

I was absolutely blown away when I started doing the research and realized that the majority of child molesters are married. "Oh my God, how sick!" I thought. When I think that a married man, a man who has an adult partner, is interested in someone's precious little daughter sexually, I literally want to throw up. He has a wife, yet his interest is for a little girl! What else might he do? What else is he capable of? My conclusion is this: anything and everything!

The more I researched, the more I learned. I started noticing all the news reports of sexual abuse. I read about molestation in daycare centers. I saw the stories of coaches, teachers, the clergy, fathers, and stepfathers guilty of abusing children. I heard of so many people in positions of authority over children who used, misused, and took advantage of their positions for their own lust and desires.

I read how these monstrous villains chose to use young children in the most heinous and vile of ways; and they do it all under the guise of love and trust. They do it with a pretense of care and compassion. Yet they do it in secrecy; and in their wake they leave young children shocked and numb. They leave these babies filled with shame and guilt. They leave these innocent, faultless victims to wonder what is wrong with them, why were they singled out for such horrible abuse by someone they loved and trusted

These monsters use the love and trust of their victims to abuse and to manipulate. They are sick and twisted and have no shame. When Nikki was in the fifth grade, the school district had some type of abuse awareness program, and she came home with a questionnaire that needed to be filled out. Jack was so bold and brazen that he sat with Nikki to complete the questionnaire, asking her questions like "Has anyone touched you inappropriately?" Her molester was doing what all molesters do best. He was manipulating the situation, and he was manipulating her. He was very good at it.

I distinctly remember a case in Ohio in which a husband had been abusing the children in his wife's daycare for years. She never knew it. Or the case in Austria, where the man imprisoned and impregnated his own daughter over the course of twenty-four years. His wife never knew. Or the sick couple in Orlando, Florida, that had children solely for the purpose of molesting them.

Then there was the 2011, high profile case of Jerry Sandusky, a retired college football coach convicted of molesting young boys over a span of fifteen years, as he organized numerous football camps and founded The Second Mile, a children's charity. Sandusky groomed his young victims for abuse. He was ultimately charged with fifty-two counts of sexual abuse.

This "grooming" is what a predator does. This pretense of love and affection; of wanting to spend time with kids because they have big hearts. They all do it. They all do lots of other things too vile for me to put in print.

Yes, as the mother, I definitely feel violated to this day.

A Prayer for a Loving Countenance

Dear Father God, we your daughters come before you now, thanking you for another day, thanking you for the ability to use our limbs, thanking you for the breath in our body, thanking you for all that you continue to do in our lives. Dear God, even in these very difficult circumstances, we shall continue to give you praise, just for who you are.

Now we come before you asking, Father, please don't let us walk away jaded, hard-hearted, and cynical. Please do not allow us to see the world only through pained and harsh lenses. Lord, this person has taken away enough from us already. Please do not let him take away our ability to love and be loved.

Lord, you created us, and although the enemy has given us an uppercut in this battle, he shall not win the war. We know the ultimate victory is in you, we know the ultimate victory is in continuing to trust and believe, continuing our lives and continuing to grow in Christ, and this can only be done with a loving countenance. This is our prayer in Jesus's name. Amen.

20. Two Wet Cats

When thou passes through the waters, I will be with thee, and through the rivers, they shall not overflow thee: when thou walkest through the fire, thou shall not be burned, neither shall the flame kindle upon thee. Isaiah 43:2 (KJV)

Have you ever seen how vulnerable and scared a wet cat is? That's what I saw the morning I walked into my daughter's high school office area. There was a flurry of activity in the office that day. It was immediately obvious that something was happening. Something big. Off to the right was the office of assistant principal, Tina Brinker.

Tina had been in the community only a short time, just a couple of years, and had become a friend. As I approached her office and peered in, I saw my daughter sitting in a chair crying. Tamirra was sitting on her lap, her eyes glassy and dazed.

Both Nikki and Tamirra are petite. They are each thin and barely weigh two hundred pounds together. I started immediately toward the girls but was stopped short when Tina left her office and came toward me. I saw nothing but the intensity in my friend's eyes. She shook her head slightly, but the message was in her eyes. Her eyes and her body language spoke volumes: "Don't."

So I didn't. I didn't say a word. I stood quietly, waiting to learn what in the world was happening. You see, it was nothing new, in fact it had become quite common for Nikki, who was fifteen years old and in the tenth grade, to call me during the school day. Her world had been turned upside down. Academics for my daughter were becoming unmanageable. Although she had previously been a solid B student, she was no longer able to focus or to concentrate.

88

Now, rather than being the attentive student she used to be, she would get passes from her teachers to go to the office. I knew she was trying to find a place to hide. She was trying to find a way to cope. She would get passes from the teachers to leave class, and she would go to the office to sit. I found out later that she was only attending a couple of classes a day.

I would take Nikki to school, reassure her that everything was going to be alright, give her a pep talk, tell her how she needs to go to school, and don't let *him* take anything else from us. I would watch her walk into the school and then immediately begin crying to the point of heaving, I couldn't get out of the school parking lot, I would lean over to the passenger side of the car and just cry my eyes out. This became one of my regular rituals.

On this particular day, when Nikki called me to come to the school, she did not see me waiting outside the office, and after a couple of minutes, Tina opened the door to usher me in. I sat down, waiting for someone to say something. It seemed an eternity before anyone spoke. I looked at Nikki, and it was obvious that she was having a total, emotional breakdown. She was in no condition to talk.

Tamirra looked at me, and I could see the absolute fear in her eyes. I can still see that pure, unadulterated terror. She had no idea what was about to happen.

Then, for just a moment, Nikki stopped crying. "Tamirra, too!" she said.

"Tamirra, too, what?" I asked, almost exasperated.

I wanted to know what in the heck was going on. Why is Tamirra sitting on Nikki's lap, why is there this air of eerie silence in the room, and why isn't Nikki in class? All of this was going through my head at the same time. Nikki and Tamirra are not that close, they know each other, and always did get along well, but that was the extent of it.

"Would somebody please tell me what's going on here...all of this was going on in mind. Finally I hear...

"He did it to Tamirra, too!"

My heart stopped. I knew what Nikki was saying. My eyes grew large, shaking my head, I sank back into the chair. I could not speak. I looked at Tamirra and Nikki as they sat hugging each other.

That dirty dog! That dirty, low-down, scum-of-the-earth dog! It was unbelievable. It was simply and utterly *unbelievable!* The same man who abused my daughter had also abused this young girl, his adopted sister.

Nikki and Tamirra now have a bond. They have a connection they never had before but will have forever more. They are connected by the same perpetrator. They were molested by the same man.

How many more are out there that we don't know about? How many little girls has he molested? I continue to ask the questions, "Why?" How could he do this? How many more young girls, young women, has this man I called my husband victimized? I think of all the foster children his mother has cared for over the years.

You see, Tamirra, although much younger than him, was adopted by Jack Reiss's mother. Legally, he and Tamirra are brother and sister. I had met Tamirra and had come to know her throughout the years of my marriage to this beast. Nikki knew her as well, and they were now attending the same high school, although they did not run in the same circle of friends.

It was purely an accident that they learned each other's story. Or perhaps it was meant to be. Because Nikki was having such a difficult time focusing on her academic work, rather than being excused to the office, she sometimes asked to be allowed to go to the library.

This particular day had been an especially difficult day for her. She'd once again been excused to the library, which is where she saw Tamirra. The conversation went something like this:

Tamirra: "Hi, Nikki."

Nikki: "Hi."

Tamirra: "How you doing?"

Nikki: "I'm not doing so good."

Tamirra: "What's wrong?"

Nikki: "I told my mom about Jack."

Tamirra: "What about him?"

Nikki: "What he's been doing to me."

Tamirra: "Has he been messing with you? Cause he's been messing with me."

Nikki: "*What*? He's been messing with you too? You've got to tell somebody!"

At that point, Nikki and Tamirra went to Tina Brinker. They told her they were being abused. Tina immediately called Child Protective Services, who then interviewed Tamirra and opened an investigation.

Nikki, my brothers, and I had already been to the police. An investigation was ongoing for Nikki's case. Tamirra eventually joined forces with Nikki, and their two cases became one.

In the end, you see, it was these two little girls, these sweet and innocent adolescents, who spoke out. It was these two fragile, little wet cats, who were vulnerable, shaking and scared, who found the courage to tell responsible adults about what had happened to them.

It was these two little girls, whom had you said "BOO!" to, either would have scurried off running. But they found the courage. They somehow found the inner fortitude to do what those who had gone before them could not or would not do.

I was so proud of them. I admired their strength and their courage, because I know if wasn't easy. I watched as these two girls stood their ground. I watched as they did not waiver. They did not change their stories, no matter how many questions they had to answer, no matter how many different angles others took in their approach to them. No matter how many questions filled with doubt came at them. No matter how they were bullied, harassed, threatened.

Tamirra was ambushed by Jack's family and beat up in the open street after the trial, because she dared to speak against him. She was shunned by his family, and was thrown to the wolves during a time you would think she would be embraced. This often happens to those who speak out and is an effective deterrent against the truth coming to the light. Tamirra did have many opportunities to recant, and then she could come back into the loving arms of the family, however she did not and her assailant was found guilty of molesting her as well as Nikki.

I'll never forget what the prosecutor said about Tamirra's situation, "children don't lie to get into trouble, they lie to get out of it". Tamirra had a troubled past, and we know that she has lied on many occasions, however the testimony she gave rang true with the detectives, the prosecutor, and ultimately the jury.

The girls remained steadfast as they both individually and collectively spoke in an open courtroom on more than one occasion. They were strong, and they were resolute when they told their stories about what a member of their own family, what Jack Reiss, had done to them.

Prayer for Our Children

Father God, in the name of your dear Son, we come before you now thanking you for the gift that you blessed us with—our children. Thank you, Father, and now we come to you on behalf of our children; they need you now, please be with them, give them the strength they need to continue to live, thrive, and survive a horrible ordeal.

Father, cause them to know that they are yet loved and loveable, and most of all that they did nothing wrong and we do not look at them any differently. Father, let them know they are not "used goods"; let them know the enemy is a liar, and don't let them go down the wrong path of drugs, self-harming behaviors, of all kinds, let them have some understanding that there are people in this world who sometimes make bad choices, and that's what happened to them. Give them your peace. In Jesus's name we pray. Amen.

21. The Research Says...

*But whoso shall offend one of these little ones which believe in me, it were better for him that a **millstone** were hanged about his neck, and that he were drowned in the depth of the sea.   Matthew 18:6 (KJV)*

The reality of sexual abuse is startling. Until it happened to us, I had absolutely no idea how prevalent, how epidemically insidious it is in our society. Until it happened to us, to my daughter and to my entire family, I had not paid as close attention as I do now.

Now I listen intently. Now I search out the facts. Now I cannot get enough information. I cannot know enough or learn enough or be aware enough. Somehow I think knowing will save us. I realize it's too late to save Nikki from her abuser. I realize it's too late to save my family from the horror and the pain we lived through.

Maybe, somehow, the facts can still save us. That's what I think as I research and learn and study. I think that if we become truly aware of this plague upon our society, if we can see if for what it really is, then we can start to accept it. We can somehow come to terms that it happened to us. Maybe knowing that it happens to so many makes it easier to bear that it happened to us.

I also pray. I *pray* that all my research and learning and study might save another little girl. It might somehow save another family, even if it's only from a tiny portion of their suffering.

Here are the facts according to the Department of Justice in a 2013 report on maltreatment:

- 26% of sexually abused victims were between twelve and fourteen years of age. An even larger group, 34% were younger than age nine.

- Nearly two million adolescents in the United States have been sexually assaulted.
- The Centers for Disease Control (CDC) estimates that one in six boys and one in four girls are sexually abused before they turn eighteen.
- Over one-third of sexual assaults take place when the victim is between the ages of twelve and seventeen.
- Eighty-two percent of adolescent victims are girls.
- Sixty-nine percent of sexual assaults on teens reported take place in a place of residence, either the victim's, the offender's or another individual's.
- Teenagers between the ages of sixteen and nineteen are three-and-a-half times more likely to be victims of rape, attempted rape, or sexual assault than those in the general population.
  - Approximately one in five high school girls' reports being physically and/or sexually abused by someone they have dated.

Prayer for Humanity

Father, in the name of Jesus we your daughters come before you on behalf of humankind. Father, we plea for this world, we cry out for kindness, for love, for gentleness, for meekness, for temperance in the land. Lord, we cry out that your people will return to you and will seek you while you may be found. We pray for those who are hungry, we pray for the fatherless, we pray for the oppressed, the used, and the abused in this world; we pray for those who are trafficked in the sex and slave industries, we pray for the teenage runaways who end up on street corners and in the pornography industry.

Father, we pray right now for those who have been molested and no longer value their own bodies and end up in the "Gentleman's Club." Lord, it's a scourge on our land, and we pray for those who have accepted and supported it right now in the name of Jesus. Father, open their eyes that they might see the grown woman was a little girl used and abused at one time. This is our prayer in Jesus's name. Amen.

22. The Disclosure

And this is the confidence that we have in him that, if we ask any thing according to his will, he heareth us: 1 John 5:14

Nikki had "disclosed." "Disclosure" is what it's called when children report that they have been sexually molested. It's such a sterile word. It's a very formal word for the difficult and frightening process of saying, "This is what happened to me. This is what this man/woman/child did to me."

The word is so very clinical. Many children who have been molested take weeks or months or, as in Nikki's case, years to find the courage to report what was done to them. Some never tell at all. And when they do, most of them reveal the awful details little by little. One at a time, they disclose little pieces of an enormous ordeal.

She had told me of the horror with which she'd dealt. The absolute horror of which I'd had no idea, but finally, after Jack was out of our home, after my daughter had suffered quietly, like the sweet, caring little girl she'd always been, she disclosed.

There is no definitive way in which a child discloses his or her abuse, but there is research, there are case studies, and there are patterns:

- Girls typically disclose more readily than boys.
- Children of school age usually tell a parent or caregiver.
- Children in their adolescent years tend to tell a trusted friend.
- Children quite young are likely to accidentally report the abuse. They don't have the vocabulary or understanding of what has happened, and so may reveal their abuse, for

example, in the way they play with a doll or even other children.

- Children who get a lot of support after they tell typically have fewer symptoms of trauma. The abuse also ends much earlier.
- Children who receive negative reactions to their disclosure often continue to suffer abuse. They are also more likely to suffer symptoms of post-traumatic stress disorder in their adult years.

It is true that children disclose in a variety of ways. Traditionally, it was believed that most children of abuse disclose gradually. It was thought that children who were abused would go through several stages as they disclosed: keeping the abuse a secret, feeling helpless and trapped, finally disclosing, and then perhaps retracting their story because they are afraid they won't be believed or in fear that they will be blamed.

Often these children must be interviewed repeatedly over a period of time before they finally overcome the fear they have of fully disclosing.

Other children disclose more rapidly. It really doesn't matter whether your child discloses gradually or all at once. What matters is that he tells his story. That he calls out for help. That he says, "This is what has happened to me."

Because when your child does that, when he tells you what is going on, when he "discloses," you can begin to help him through a process that will determine whether he survives the ordeal and becomes whole once again or whether he does not.

Ezekiel 36:26 tells of how the Lord can take a stony heart and make it a heart of flesh. I wanted Him to do that for me. I wanted Him to soften my stony heart. My daughter's molester had taken enough from us. I did not want to give another inch. I knew that becoming mean, hateful and bitter would have been playing right into the enemy's hand.

So my heart's greatest desire at this time was that I might walk away from this experience with that heart of flesh rather than with a heavy, bitter heart of stone. It felt as though it would be so easy to walk away with nothing left inside me but the coldness and the harshness that threatened to consume me. Certainly anyone and everyone- those I knew and those I had yet to meet- would understand. Certainly I'd be given a pass: "She's suffered so much," they would say. "Her daughter was sexually abused by someone she loved and trusted."

All those I encountered would shake their heads sadly. They'd understand. They'd forgive me for the hardness my heart now held.

However, I did *not* want this to happen to me, and I did not want any of my own heaviness or bitterness to infect my daughter. Therefore, even before I consciously knew the importance of what I was asking, one of my first prayers after Nikki disclosed went something like this: "God please don't let me walk away jaded, hard-hearted and cynical. Please do not allow me to see the world only through pained and harsh lenses. Lord, this man has taken away enough from us already. Please do not let him take away my ability to love and be loved."

I know so many people who have let the harsh and bitter winds of life leave them resentful and cold. I've known so many people in my life who walk around with a chip on their shoulder. They are always mad. They are always angry. They always have something mean to say. These harsh and bitter people are very hard to be around. You see them coming one way, and you want to run the other. I did not want to be like that. I did not want this hard, hurtful episode to define us forever and ever. Amen.

I prayed and asked the Lord to keep my heart pliable. I wanted my heart to remain soft and useable in His hands. I asked that He keep my heart and soul soft like play dough so that He could continue to mold, shape, bend and use me according to His will. I prayed that I not become hard and stiff, unable to see the freshness in a spring day, unable to see the beauty in a rose about to bloom, unable to appreciate the breaking of a new summer day. I wanted still to be able to smell the freshness of the first snow of the season and laugh when I was drenched in the rain and looked a hot mess.

I wanted to be able to sit in the yard on summer nights and simply enjoy the sounds, sights and smells of being alive. I wanted to enjoy cuddling up with my favorite book while sitting at the beach and listening to the sound of the waves. Most of all, I wanted, still, to enjoy just sitting in the sun and feeling it on my face. You see, I wanted so badly, still, to be able to feel!

You can only feel if your heart is pliable, if it is soft and has blood pumping through it. You can only feel if you can love and give of yourself, expecting nothing in return. This is who I was before this nightmare began and this is who I am today; this is the true me. I knew that if I stopped loving and giving freely for fear of being hurt again, then I would stop living. I knew that the enemy would have won.

I knew if I allowed myself to cower in fear and simmer in an angry hurt that I would turn into someone other than who I am.

At that point I would have put on a mask; I would be hiding away and denying my true identity. I would have put myself in a prison of sorts and become something other than who I truly am and who I was truly meant to be. I refused to do that. I continue today to refuse to do that. I am a loving, giving person. I like being a loving, giving person. I shall continue to be just that.

It's funny. Not funny *ha ha*, but funny *interesting*. When you choose to be who you are, it is the most freeing feeling in the world. It's exhilarating. It is thrilling and awesome. It simply feels good.

Perhaps the very best thing about choosing to be who you are is that you are honoring the God who created you. I am the way I am because God made me that way, and I love this person God made me to be. I like to give. I like to love. I like to be kind to people. I like to go out of my way to help those around me.

So when I prayed my prayer for a heart of flesh, I was asking God to help me continue to be the me that He'd so lovingly created. I was asking Him to honor me by returning me to who I'd been before. I prayed this prayer so desperately: I wanted to go back to being *me*.

As mothers of children that have been abused, we must, along with making sure our children survive their own horror, find a way to survive ours. We must find a way back to the women we once were.

So we must ask, "Now what?" How does the mom find her way back? How does she keep *herself* together? How does she deal with her family? How does she deal with her community, her workplace, her church and her circle of friends? How, she wonders, will *she* be viewed? Will she be blamed? Will others point and whisper that she somehow allowed this to happen? Will others assign to her the guilt she's trying so hard not to assign herself? Will she forever be bitter and carry the stigmas of being the mother that *let* her child be abused?

Some people, there is no doubt, will believe that she knew about the abuse. That she knew but turned a blind eye. Some will begin to whisper the heinous rumors that yes, indeed, she knew. She knew and did nothing to stop it. But you must, I repeat, you *must* know in your heart that what they say, even what they may believe, is not at all what is most important. What is most important is what you know and what you feel about yourself.

You must also know that you cannot be all things to all people. You must take some time for yourself. You cannot continually to give without setting aside time for you. When you are exhausted, when you are drained and feel at a complete loss for where to turn, this is the most opportune time for the enemy to come at you again.

When he has you focused on everything and everyone except yourself, he will come at you to cause you pain. He will demand you question all you've done and all you've not done. He will take you in your time of distracted anguish and he will try to strike, yet again, at your soul. Remember that in Genesis 3:1 (ESV), we are told, "Now the serpent was more crafty than any beast of the field that the Lord God had made." God has warned us that the enemy is cunning and subtle and he will strike us at our lowest point. He will strike while we are hurting.

One of the best ways to defend yourself against this evil that has crept into your life is to go on the offensive. By picking up this book, you have done exactly that. You have determined to build yourself up. You have chosen to arm yourself with the information you need to survive the horror of what you have endured. You are entering into community with other women like yourself who have walked through this darkness and come out the other side to see the sun shine once again.

Prayer for Revelations Everywhere

Father, Father, Father, we are here before you now in unison, now that we know what we didn't know prior, and as hard as it is, we are ever so thankful to have the truth of what took place. Lord, you said in your word the truth will make you free. Lord, it hurts too.

Father, we ask right now in the name of Jesus that little boys and girls across this nation and everywhere that are being touched will tell somebody that will care, listen, and take action on their behalf! Father, we know that our children will be better off not having to hide the secret any longer.

Thank you for the freedom, and we want the other children to have that same freedom, no longer walking around in shame and secrecy. Lord, we pray right now in the name of Jesus for freedom, for truth, and for revelation; shine your light on dark situations everywhere. In Jesus's name we pray. Amen.

23. Strength to Deliver

For I know the plans I have for you, declares the LORD, plans to prosper you and not to harm you, plans to give you hope and a future Jeremiah 29:11

I was hurting. I was broken and devoid of all feeling. Yet I was determined to do whatever needed to be done to help my daughter heal. I wanted her to be whole again. I so desperately wanted the true Nikki to blossom and to be able to step forth into the woman God intended for her to be.

As much as I tried and as hard as I prayed that she be able to put the horror of her molestation behind her, I saw that she was not coping. In fact, she was not doing well at all. So I did the only thing I could think to do. I enrolled her in counseling.

She met with her counselor a couple of times, but I could tell that it really wasn't making much of a difference for her. It simply, and obviously, was not helping. When I asked her what the problem was, her response was that the counselor was too old. I remember her saying, "It's like talking to Grandma."

But I refused to give up. I knew Nikki needed to talk to a professional. All my research and reading had convinced me she needed to talk with someone who knew how to talk back. I immediately spoke with the counseling office. I felt bad about having to ask for a younger counselor and apologized to the older woman Nikki had been seeing. But this was not about the counselor and her feelings. It was about Nikki. It was about giving my daughter a chance to heal. I needed Nikki to be comfortable talking with someone who was available for *her* needs.

We did find another counselor with whom Nikki seemed more comfortable sharing her feelings and her struggles. She attended these counseling sessions on a regular basis for about six months. However, there came a time with this younger professional when Nikki, once again, did not want to go back.

Now I understand. I'm sure she was tired of talking about the molestation. She was tired of living through it again and again. We were at the time going through the trial. She was reliving it again and again in a public forum. She'd had enough.

You see, when molestation occurs, it takes over your life. In every moment of every day, you must live and breathe again what happened. You really do need to find an escape. You need to find room to breathe freely. You need to find somewhere, anywhere, to be a regular person.

I found that somewhere to breathe freely at church. That was my place to run to for some sense of purpose and normalcy. I was so destroyed as a person, yet this was the *one* place I could let go of some of the pain I was feeling, so that is where I went—as often as I could.

I was at the church on weekdays from 11am to noon every chance I could be there. I was at the church on Tuesday evenings for our regular prayer and Bible study. I was at the church on Friday evenings for intercessors prayer, and I was at the church on Sunday mornings for Sunday school and then our regular Sunday morning worship.

I was seeking God as I never had before. Not only did I want to hear from him-the desire was definitely there-I felt as though I *needed* to hear from him. I was possessed with a need to have Him touch my life, to hear my prayers and to begin to heal me. NO ONE else could speak to my situation. NO ONE else could heal my broken heart. NO ONE could possibly understand what I was going through.

I knew that I had to find a way to release my own pain. I knew that I had to find a way to return to my former self. But more than ever, I knew the only way that could happen was somehow making my daughter whole. NO ONE on this earth could heal my daughter, and NO ONE could repair and restore her inner soul, which is where the breach occurred. She needed to be healed as a person; she needed restoration. She so needed to be returned to her former state, to the person she'd been before the molestation. She so needed to be "normal."

Who does a mother go to for that? Who does a mother ask to return her daughter to a time prior to her being touched by a sick, twisted, and perverted man? Who does a mother go to so her daughter can be returned to "normal? What human being can provide that?

I understood that Nikki could go on with her life; that she would live and grow and maybe even experience joy. But what I needed was for *nothing* to stand in her way. I needed for her to have no fears or uncertainty or emotional scars. I needed for her to resolve the issues she was bearing. I needed her to carry NO BAGGAGE because of what took place to hinder her future.

That's why I so desperately wanted to trade places with my daughter. I wanted to carry her guilt and her shame so that she could go on with her life and be free of all of it. I wanted her to shed every remaining morsel of what she had lived through. As much as I wanted this for my daughter, I too, was carrying so much shame and guilt that my feet felt as if they were stuck in the mud.

It always came back to this: How in the world did you, her mother, her primary caregiver, allow this to happen? How did you, an intelligent woman, not see what was taking place in your own home? How did you allow that man to hoodwink and bamboozle you to the point that your own precious daughter was being molested? For crying out loud, *how* did you not pick up on *anything*?

Then it would come back to this: Why wouldn't she tell? Wouldn't my daughter tell me if some man, any man, tried to touch her? Of course she would! I'm a good mother! Aren't I?

Okay, I would end up telling myself, so maybe I'm not a great mother. I'm *not* a stay-at-home mom. I don't spend enough time with my children. I don't play with them enough. I don't bake enough cookies with them. I didn't read enough with them.

I would go through all the regular guilt trips working mothers go through, but I would then insist to myself, I am a good mother! I love and care for my daughter. I provide for her. I teach her right from wrong. I have brought her up in the church, to know and to love the Lord. I take her on regular, fun family vacations. We've been to Disney World twice, and we've traveled on many occasions to Maryland, where our extended family and her father lives. We've stayed in a log cabin in Virginia, traveled to the Gatlinburg Mountains in Tennessee.

Lord knows, I think the world of her! I've done all I can do to love and to teach and to nurture my most precious little girl. I must say it over and over and over again, even if only to convince myself. I am a good mother!

Prayer For Our Daughters' Futures

Father God, we come before you right now thanking you once again for all that you have done. We thank you for your goodness, for your mercy, for your loving kindness toward us. We thank you, God, for our daughters. Thank you, God, for the plans you have for them are good and not evil, to give them a future and a hope. For they shall live and not die, and declare the goodness of the Lord.

Thank you that even in this trying time you are still God, and you are still good. Lord, we shall continue to talk and tell our children of how good you are, how great you are through every situation, trial, test, circumstance. Lord, we want to be counted worthy.

Yes, Lord, we will remain faithful—through it all we shall still bless your name. The Lord is my light and my salvation, whom shall I fear? I will teach this to my child, to trust in the Lord, we will sing hymns, and meditate on your goodness. This is our prayer in Jesus's name. Amen.

24. Fire in His Eyes

Be sober, be vigilant; because your adversary the devil, as a roaring lion, walketh about, seeking whom he may devour: 1Peter 5:8 (KJV)

We had been in the court process for a little over three months and were back and forth with some trial dates already. There was a lot of lawyer finagling going on.

We live in a small town of about 40,000 people, of which about 2,000 are African-American. We are a part of that small, community. We all know one another. We see each other in the local stores and at the high school ballgames. We see each other at church. When something happens to one of us, we all know.

Because we were an intricate part of this small, fairly close-knit community, everybody knew about our case. No matter where Nikki went, no matter where I went, we had to deal with an entire community who knew.

By this time, my eldest son Jared, who is seven years older than Nikki had graduated from college and moved to the Washington D.C. Metropolitan area. He was living close to his father and my brothers, and working for NASA. Jared had graduated from college with his Bachelor's degree in computers and, not because there was no bed but by his own choice, was sleeping on the floor. He was so ambitious he told his aunt he did not want to get too comfortable living with someone else.

Over three months had passed since Nikki had revealed to me her abuse. It was March 2, 2007, and I finally knew I could tell Jared what had taken place. I had been praying a lot about the right time to tell him, knowing I needed to do so. It had been difficult talking to him the last two to three months because I constantly had to be on guard with what I said and how I sounded when I spoke to him. I did not want to let the "cat out of the bag," so our conversations were centered on the surface: "How's the weather? How's your job? How are things going?" And our answers were the same, "I've been real busy. Everybody is doing fine." We had all the surface, cursory types of conversations you have to keep from really talking to someone.

Jared was and is very athletic; he's six foot three and weighs about 250 pounds. He works out regularly in the gym and has the physique of a football player. In fact, he was a football player, but due to a torn ACL during high school, he began walking down another career path.

Jared has plans to be an entrepreneur, just like his father. He has seen what financial success looks like, and he wants that success for himself.

Over the objections of my family who wanted to tell Jared earlier, I picked this day to finally tell my son what had happened to his younger sister.

I knew I had to tell him personally. I knew I couldn't keep it from him forever, yet I also knew that I needed to tell him at the right time. I was not sure what his reaction would be, and I did not want him to jeopardize his future. Jack Reiss had already done enough damage to my family. There was no way I was going to tell Jared about Nikki's molestation without considerable thought and preplanning. I knew my son would be furious.

I knew beyond a shadow of a doubt that Jared was going to want to get his hands around Jack Reiss's neck to choke the life from him. I also knew he was big enough and strong enough to do exactly that. I could easily see Jared doing whatever he needed to do to get here. I knew he would drive the five hundred miles enraged, fuming, and fantasizing about the various ways he would inflict pain on Jack Reiss for what had been done to his sister and for the pain Jared himself had endured while Jack was in our home. Certainly there was no love lost there. Jared had always told us that Jack was not what he purported himself to be. It turned out Jared was the only one who was right after all.

With all this in mind, I knew it was now safe to tell Jared what Jack Reiss had done. Jared couldn't do anything; he couldn't get to him. So I told him about the sexual molestation. Most importantly I told him that Jack Reiss had been arrested and was in jail.

Jared said some things that day that were very difficult for me to hear. He repeated over and over, "MOM—I TOLD YOU! I told you! NOBODY WOULD LISTEN TO ME!"

I can't tell you how many times Jared said, "I told you!" He spoke first from shock and disbelief, and then his words turned into anger and rage, fury and hate all rolled up into one. It was in that moment that I knew I'd made the right decision to wait to tell him until he couldn't do anything. The worse thing that could happen to Nikki at that point would be to have her brother in jail for assault and battery against her molester.

I had been dealing with this for the past three or four months. I had been able to process a lot. Jared, though, had not. This was all brand new information for him, and the bottom line was that *he had been right all along about Jack Reiss's character.*

On the following day I received a call from my sister-in-law. She said Jared was so mad that she couldn't even describe it. She'd never seen anything like it. I told her that I know what seeing Jared so angry is like. "You saw fire in his eyes," I said.

"Yes," she agreed. "That's what it was. It was fire in his eyes."

I told her that I knew. I told her I had heard the fire in his voice and that I was so glad he was not here.

I certainly understood my son's feelings; I had imagined doing some vile things to Jack Reiss myself.

If you have other children in your home, know that they will be affected. Know that, perhaps, they know, or at least suspect, what your daughter has worked so hard to hide. Children are smart. They are intuitive. They are paying attention to what is happening in your home and to the family dynamic, even when you may be too busy to do so yourself.

You must find a way to make it through this poisonous thing that has affected not just your daughter, not just you, but your entire family. Please understand that. This is not a situation you should try to hide from, nor should you try to shield your other children from having to face what has happened to their sibling. You must confront what has happened, and you must allow your daughter's brothers and sister to confront it as well. It is only through confronting the evil that you can reduce its power. It is only through confronting the evil that you can make it go away.

I cannot stress enough the importance of having this discussion with your children. I implore you to make this a family affair. You can discuss what has happened in age-appropriate terms. You do not have to reveal the grittiest of details. But you must talk. And you must let your children respond. You must let them ask questions.

One of the most powerful healing steps for my family were the family meetings we began to hold, my extended family included. We would go into a huddle. We had sideline chats, sometimes it meant long distance calls, sometimes this meant chain calls, sometimes it was just the three of us, it varied over the course of time. Because this was a struggle that involved us all, we all were involved in coping. We discussed. We talked. And I know that allowing all of my children to vocalize their questions and their fears helped immensely in the healing process of us all. We are a family.

You, too, are a family. There is a strength in numbers, and there is a strength in the family bond. I urge you not to overlook the importance of that—for all of you.

You owe it to yourself to feel who you are at this point in time. You owe it to yourself to recognize your own needs, to take a break when you need to, to get recharged. And then you owe it to yourself to return to your life, to take your life back.

Not giving up your family is a part of this return to your former self. This is the family you love. It is your family, and you are a mother bear that will fiercely protect her family at all costs. You will rise up and growl and say, "Enough! Enough suffering. Enough pain. Enough victimization."

Right now, this moment, may be the most difficult and painful time for you. But I want you to know that you can and you will get through this. You must! You must survive not only for your daughter's sake, but for your sake as well. You deserve to be whole again. You deserve to be complete and happy and content and at peace. And you will be. You will heal. The shattered pieces of who you are will meld back into a whole.

You too may have to experience this, where you are not just dealing with the incest itself, but all that goes along with it. As this type of violation is not the kind that is done in the open, it's not the kind people readily talk about like a death, yet for you, for your family, for your child, a death, a loss has occurred nonetheless, however unspoken it may be. All of you will need to find new ways to cope with the fragments and the shattered pieces that are left behind.

My suggestion to you is to pick up every fragment that you can, and hold on to it. You may not have the energy, the time, nor the courage to put the pieces together, at this time, but there will come a time, when you will want to put those pieces back together again. There will come a time when you will be able to look at those fragments and not look at them solely as fragments, but you will be able to see the beauty in them as they are and know that almighty God in his infinite wisdom can take those fragments, if you give them to him, and mend those pieces together, and bring life out of death, he can breathe on you, on your daughter, on your family, on and in your Spirit,

Yes those bones can live again, but not know, not until you're ready, not until you have went into those deep dark lonely, lowly recess of your mind, heart and soul. Yes it is tough, yes it is lonely, and yes you will never be the same person you were before this occurred, yet because you have made the decision to not go it alone, you and your daughter will be stronger, wiser, more compassionate, and like clay ready to be molded for good works in the "Masters' Hand."

I have written this book as an act of obedience. God told me too. As a matter of fact he REQUIRED that I do this. He said this book must be published, and I was being disobedient in taking so long to complete the assignment.

Prayer for Family Members

Dear Heavenly Father, we, your mothers, come to your Throne of Grace with our hearts full. Father, we are full when we think about how faithful you have been to us in this state of affairs. You have did just what you promised. You have stood by us. You have stood by our daughter. You have stood by our family. Father, we ask right now that you do not let this situation cause a root of bitterness to be lodged in any of my family members' hearts. You said we are not ignorant of the enemy's devices.

Even now, Father, our male family members want to take action; most men want to "do" something. Father, we ask right now in the name of Jesus that what my family members "do" is be a support to my daughter. Let my family members use wisdom in their actions and their communications, let not the enemy have an opportunity to twist or use anything my family member does against them in the end. Vengeance is mine, saith the Lord. You said you would repay. This is our prayer in Jesus's name. Amen.

25. Brothers on Duty

Learn to do right! Seek justice, relieve the oppressed, and correct the oppressor. Defend the fatherless, plead for the widow. Isaiah 1:17 (AMP)

I am the only girl and the youngest of three siblings. I have two older brothers whom I cherish and look up to. We have a fantastic relationship and always have. My brothers are each married to beautiful, God-fearing women who are great mothers and supportive wives. We help one another, look out for one another, and encourage one another. And although we all have our own trials, ebbs and flows, we give each other room to be who we are.

I can count on my brothers and my sisters-in-law whenever I need help or encouragement, a friend, or a good kick in the pants. That's the way our parents and our extended family raised us. We have all raised our children in the same way.

It is Christmas, 2006. Kenny is the eldest of my brothers, five years my senior. Ronnie is three years older than I. They each have already been informed of Nikki's situation. My mother knew nothing, and my father had just passed away.

The boys returned home to Michigan from Maryland after the holiday and went downstairs with Nikki and me to talk with her about going to the police.

Nikki kept saying that Jack is a "good guy," which made our skin crawl. I knew, however, it was the Stockholm syndrome playing out with my daughter as the victim. I knew it's often what happens. The hostage expresses empathy and sympathy for his or her captors.

Later my brothers told me they'd had a conversation with Jack prior to our being married. They had talked with him, wanting to ensure themselves that I was and would be loved. They told him that he had better "treat me right." Kenny still talks about how he had no idea he needed to say something about Nikki. He had no idea Jack needed to be cautioned to treat his new step-daughter right as well.

Ronnie and Kenny tried to deprogram Nikki. They tried to get her to see that a "good guy" does not molest little girls. A "good guy" does not abuse people. A "good guy" does not pretend to be a Christian when he is showing pornography to little girls.

Nikki was absolutely, unequivocally, opposed to the idea of going to the authorities and all that it entailed. Kenny and Ronnie talked with her about what Jack Reiss did. They told her she didn't have to do anything. She could simply hear what the police said and learn what the procedures are.

Ronnie was supposed to return to Maryland the next day, and I remember him saying to Nikki, "You are more important. I can stay here for you."

On Saturday, December 26, 2006, with my brothers Kenny and Ronnie, Nikki and I went to the Port Huron Police Department.

You see, brothers do have wings. My brothers were like warring angels for me and for Nikki. They did that day what no one else could do.

Nikki would not have listened to *anyone* else no one else had been consistent in her life like her uncles were. I will always and forever be indebted to my brothers for loving my daughter and for standing by her. They were there when her father was not. They were there when no one else was. Because my brothers were there, she knew she was loved. She knew she was still Nikki. She knew that nothing had changed in how they saw her.

I picked up my Bible as we walked out the door to go to the police station, and I read Psalm 27:1 (ESV): "The Lord is my Light and my

Salvation; whom shall I fear? The Lord is the defense of my Life; whom shall I dread"

The last verse, "Wait for the LORD: be strong and let your heart take courage.

That was my battle cry as I prepared to go to war. I knew it was time. The fight was about to begin.

It was a quiet ride to the police station. Everyone must have been lost in thought, each of us lost in our own imaginations. When we arrived at the police station, Ronnie and Kenny talked alone to an officer.

Later I found out that they told the officer they believed their niece had been molested but that she was not ready to talk. They explained we were there to learn the process, to learn what to do next.

We all went into a room, and the officer talked in very general terms. I remember looking at Nikki, who had her game face on. She was not about to say anything. She had dutifully come and was going to sit and listen to whatever was said. But it was quite obvious that she had already made up her mind. She was looking for the first exit out.

The officer took Nikki aside and talked to her in private. We all looked at each other and then sat for five minutes with wonder on our faces. Would anything come of this? Would she cooperate? Why in the world does she believe he's a "good guy"? "Hasn't he," we all sat in bewilderment and thought, "done a number on her?"

You see, Jack Reiss had cased the joint. "Casing the joint" is the terminology a thief or a burglar uses in the process of inspecting—or looking over—the next heist, the next big score. In the case of a child molester, it's their next victim. Child molesters are known for being highly manipulative. They are charismatic. They portray themselves as "one of the boys," as someone who is always ready to lend a hand.

This is one of the things that makes this crime so insidious. Those who know the perpetrator as a "good guy" never know the reason for the good deeds. The good deeds are only a way for the perpetrator to get what he wants. And what the molester wants is a child to molest.

Jeremiah says that the "heart is deceitfully wicked." Jeremiah 17:9 (KJV) how were we to know?

So you have a victim stating what this "good guy" has done; and you have those he DID NOT victimize making judgments based on their limited knowledge, and I had my beautiful daughter Nikki, a victim of a horrible abuse, telling us her abuser was a "good guy."

When Nikki came out, there was no expression on her face. I walked away with her so the officers could talk with my brothers.

We waited for a moment, and then we all went home. Nikki let it be known that she had not changed her mind, although she did say she would consider moving forward. That was movement. That was progress!

I found out later that the officer had told my brother he believed Nikki. He believed she'd been molested.

Prayer for Support

Father God, we come to you in the name of Jesus. You have been good, you have been kind; truly your mercies are new every morning. Father, you have been a friend to the fatherless, to the weary, and the fainthearted in sending support to your mothers. Father, the support you have sent may have come in the way of brothers, sisters, cousins, parents, church family, or community members. Father, some sent cards of support, some sent flowers of support, some called to encourage us during this difficult time, some see us out and about in the community and offer words of encouragement.

We just want to say thank you, Father, for sending us your people who strengthen the feeble hands at just the right time; when we are weak, then you are strong. You know what we have need of, and you continue to show yourself strong in our lives. Thank you, thank you, thank you—if we had ten thousand tongues we couldn't thank you enough for sending us the Aarons and the Hurs to hold up our arms when we were too weak to win the battle. This is our prayer, in Jesus's name. Amen.

26. To Trial or Not to Trial

The entrance of thy words giveth light; it giveth understanding unto the simple. Psalm 119:130 (KJV)

If any of you lack wisdom, let him ask of God, that giveth to all men liberally, and upbraideth not; and it shall be given him. James 1:5 (KJV)

The decision to prosecute or not to prosecute your child's perpetrator is an extremely involved decision with many varying and complex factors. Each and every case must be looked at for the specific merits of that individual case. The age of the child and his or her ability to give testimony must be evaluated. All the variables that can and will transpire will your daughter be able to stand up to the rigors of a protracted legal entanglement?

These are the types of questions you will need to consider, with the help of trusted family friends, perhaps clergy. Please understand this means with the investigation, the Child welfare system, the prosecutors, and the scrutiny your daughter will receive from family, friends, and the community. The number of variables are endless, such as your daughters' mental stability and her memory of the events.

Children simply do not tell what happened to them all at once, the disclosure process is bit by bit. They test the waters to see if and how you handled the piece of information they have already given you prior to giving you additional information

The defense attorney's across the country use this as a defense tactic---"Why didn't you say this part at first, or you didn't tell us this at the initial questioning, why are you adding this now?"

All this and more became apparent during our infamous legal process when we decided to take Jack Reiss to trial.

Making this decision was one of the earliest and most important decisions that we made.

The counsel I received early on was not to go to trial. I was very tempted to take this advice. I was concerned about my daughter. I did not want Nikki to have to go through the embarrassment of a trial. I did not want her to endure one more moment of anything. And while I took the counsel under advisement, in the end, as her parent, I had to do what I felt was best for her.

It was my belief that it would be the best for her to be able to look her abuser in the eye and let it be known, "This is what happened to me. This is what you did to me. This is what you exposed me to on a regular basis. I was a child, and I trusted you. I looked up to you, and you betrayed my trust." I wanted her to be able to stand up straight and tall and openly accuse her abuser.

I also felt it was Nikki's responsibility to let it be known what happened to her so that no other little girl would be as unwittingly exposed as she was. I must reiterate that I do not believe Nikki was Jack Reiss's first victim. Again I stress that that is simply not the way child molesters work. They have many, many victims before they are finally discovered. There are many, many victims who suffer before any speak out and/or before any are believed.

I clearly remember the day that Nikki said she was ready to go talk to the detective. She had finally realized just how badly she had been used and abused. She was mad and sad all at the same time. She was both heart-broken and furious. Did she want justice? She absolutely did.

If you are a mother trying to make this decision for yourself and for your child, you will need to weigh all the variables. I ask that you have no illusions as to how our justice system works.

In her book, **Predators and Child Molesters**, Robin Sax lists ten of the most common defenses used in child sexual abuse cases as follows:

1. The child is lying because of the delay in reporting
2. The child is lying because she has disclosed more and more as time has passed
3. The child is lying because she minimized, denied, or recanted the allegations.
4. The child misperceived or misunderstood the defendant's behavior/actions
5. The child has a history of poor behavior and therefore cannot be trusted or believed
6. The child was coached by the other parent, as there is a divorce/custody case going on.
7. The child was coached and bullied by overzealous prosecutors, police, advocates, or other members of the multidisciplinary team.
8. The child fantasized or dreamed about what happened
9. The defendant is a good guy—an upstanding member of the community, an involved parent, with no prior record, etc.
10. The child is lying to get attention or because the rules of the house are too strict.

Please make no mistake about the court process. It was not easy. It was a very long, very difficult process that was extended over the course of a year.

In the end, Jack Reiss was convicted of all nine of the counts he was charged with—five count for Nikki and four for his adopted sister—had he been found innocent by the jury, the girls would have still done the right thing. They stood up and they told the truth; and by so doing, they stopped him. By having the courage and emotional fortitude to tell the truth, they laid the ground work to bring his perverted crimes to an end. Had he been found innocent this time, the next time, because with child molesters there is always a next time, he would most likely be convicted.

I really think that we as a nation are going to have to change the way we think about trying child molesters. Although a verdict of guilty is the end goal, we need to be concerned about more than simply getting a conviction. I believe we must start leaving a paper trail. We must create the records that will stand as proof of a pattern. This kid said he touched him. This kid said he touched her. And this kid said the same thing.

We are also going to have to shift the shame from the victim to the perpetrator, which we are not doing effectively. I'm not sure how it can be done, but we must somehow make it easier for the victims. They, after all, are not the ones who've done anything wrong. They are the victims.

The case of Jerry Sandusky during his tenure at Penn State University brings to mind the number of years someone with a "good reputation" for helping kids can get away with molesting children. Because he had that good reputation, because he'd worked charitably—or so it appeared—with youth for so long, he was able to deny what he had done. He was allowed to do what he did, and it got swept under the rug. Perpetrators are preying on our children, and it is being cleaned up. It is time that we as a society say, "ENOUGH."

Prayer for Decisions

Father God, in the name of Jesus we come before you now on behalf of this mother who is trying to make a very important decision. Father, who knows what is best for her child, what is best for the family, and what is best for the next child down the road. Give this mother wisdom, Father, giver her courage, give her strength, fortitude, determination, and knowledge so that she can be comfortable firm and committed with her decision, Father.

Teach us not to waiver to the left or to the right but to stand flat foot, and keep our face like a flint as we look to you, the author and the finisher of our faith. We stand with this mother in her decision to do what you give her to do. This is our prayer in Jesus's name. Amen.

27. 100 % Family Support is *Not* Necessary

And God is able to bless you abundantly, so that in all things at all times, having all that you need, you will abound in every good work.
2 Corinthians 9:8 (NIV)

I would really like to tell you that my family was all aghast, that they were in awe and shock and that *everyone* in my family came together and threw their support behind Nikki and me. I would like to tell you that.

But the truth of the matter is that was *not* my experience. This is what I have gained from that awful time and what I want you to gain from my experience. You very well may not have all of your family supporting you. Even though they should. Even though they could.

You are going to have to deal with the facts as they are, and I had to deal with the facts as they were. I had 98% of my family's support. Those who did not support me and did not support Nikki— whatever their reasons were—were not my concern. I had to do what I had to do for myself and my child. Nothing and NOBODY else mattered.

Almost everyone in my family reached out to me, my daughter, and to my mother. Nearly my entire family reached out—with the exception of a couple of extended family members. It was necessary to let all the fringe inconsequential things go by the way side—WHO CARES! It's not important and you are not going to change who people are anyway.

I was not going to deal with any family conflicts or dramas. I was not going to get sidelined or side-tracked by distractions that *were not relevant*. What people thought of me and my situation was just that—their thoughts. I was not about to ask, beg, plead or perform tricks for anyone. Did it hurt? You bet your bottom dollar it did. Did it stop anything for me or for Nikki? It stopped NOTHING.

Your job as a mother is to be that—a mother. Yours is not to soothe anyone else, not to allay anyone else's concerns, not to reach out to extended family that has always been at arm's length anyway. Your job is to be the best mother to your daughter that you can be, and it is to protect yourself during this fragile time at all costs.

Did it hurt? You bet your bottom dollar it did. Did it stop anything for me or for Nikki? It stopped NOTHING.

Your job as a mother is to be that—a mother. Yours is not to soothe anyone else, not to allay anyone else's concerns, not to reach out to extended family that has always been at arm's length anyway. Your job is to be the best mother to your daughter that you can be, and it is to protect yourself during this fragile time at all costs.

Keep at a distance those people who are not working for you even if they are your family members. Those in my family who were always on the fringes asked for information from others; they wanted reports. "What is happening?" they asked. But they never offered to Nikki or to me as much as a kind word at any time during the entire ordeal. It was remarkable!

Time after time, I would get calls from family, from the east coast to the west coast, asking if the others—my fringe family- had offered any assistance. Had they offered encouragement or information during the trial? Had they offered any help at all? The answer is that some offered nothing. They didn't reach out. They didn't phone. Not once. Nothing.

Sometimes, distance is a blessing. You as a mother have enough to deal with without the extras that come with asinine questions and false concern.

This is not a good time to deal with fringe family issues. It is not a time to concern yourself with why does Aunt Sally not like me and why does Uncle Fred favor Mike over Billy? Let all the fringe, immaterial family concerns go by the wayside. WHO CARES? It's not important. You are not going to change who people are. Your focus and energy must be on the issue at hand. You must focus on what must be done. You really don't want to go down a path trying to deal with family issues that will lead you nowhere.

The majority of the time when you have a family member standing outside looking in—he or she has a personal, unresolved deep-seated issue which has nothing to do with you anyway. This chaotic time in your life and in the life of your family is just an outlet to allow his or her issue to surface. I urge you not to fall for the trap. Don't succumb; don't take the bait. Just remember that you don't have to have 100 percent of your family's support to do what must be done.

The majority of times in life, you won't have nor do you need to have 100 percent of anything to do the right thing. Yet you still must do what is right. If possible, however, you must extend this strength, this determination to do what is right out to your extended family. They will know something has happened. They will know something is wrong.

Ask Uncle Charley to talk to Aunt Sue, who will tell Cousin Bill. Talk. Let them know and let them talk. And most of all, let your daughter know, not only with your words but with your actions, that she will not be treated differently by anyone in your family. When the family gets together, let her know that she and the horrible thing she has endured will not be the focus of family gatherings. Let her know that the entire family is here to support her.

Be gentle. Your daughter may not want to talk about what has happened to everyone. In fact, she probably *won't* want to talk to anyone. What she will want more than anything is to know how her extended family will treat her. How will they *see* her? She will peer into their eyes wondering what she'll see looking back. Will it be love? Or will it be disgust? What will she see in the eyes of her brothers, sisters, cousins, aunts and uncles? Will she see love? Or pity? Will she be treated the same? Will this completely new and somewhat foreign person she has become, this person who has suffered sexual abuse, be accepted? These are the questions that will haunt your daughter as she struggles to come to terms with what has happened.

The answer to these questions, the way in which your extended family treats your daughter is *pivotal* to her recovery. She needs to know, above all else, if she will be the center and focus of attention because of what she has endured? Or will her family treat her as they always have?

Prayer for Offense

Father God, in the name of Jesus we your daughters, the mothers come before you once again, because as your children we have the right to come to the Throne of Grace where we can find help in this our time of need. Father, we come now with a heavy heart, hurt for our daughter who has been damaged, hurt for ourselves, hurt for our family, here we are in damage control mode, and our family member, whom we expected to be a help, has caused more hurt, more harm, and more anxiety.

Father, we don't have time to deal with this. So we give this to you and say it's too much for us; you know the situation, Father, you know our heart's condition. Father, cleanse our hearts so that this offense does not set up shop in our spirit and cause a rift in our family. Father, although this has hurt us too, we offer it up to you as a sweet smelling sacrifice, you know the what and the why; Father, you have permission to deal with my heart; I ask that you do the same for my family member whom I love. In Jesus's name we pray. Amen.

28. Thank you Lord for the Victory

So David went to Baal Perazim, and David defeated them there; and he said, "The LORD has broken through my enemies before me, like a breakthrough of water." 2 Samuel 5:20 (NKJV)

In April of 2008, Jack was convicted on two counts of criminal sexual conduct in the first degree against children under the age of thirteen. He was found guilty of the rape of my daughter Nikki, who at the time the molestation began, was his eight-year-old stepdaughter. He was found guilty of raping Tamirra, his adopted sister. He was also convicted of six other child abuse charges.

The year of the trial took on a sense of the unreal. It was as though we lived it, but somehow didn't really. Although so much of it seems a blur, we endured this period of our lives the best we could. Nikki and I became obsessed with the television drama *Law & Order: Special Victims Unit.* We planned our nights around that program. Every week we looked forward to another episode, searching for something similar to what we were ourselves going through.

We needed to connect with something that might explain what we were dealing with. Our time together in front of the TV watching that show became a time and place in which we found a lot of common ground. We didn't talk much during the show. We sat in silence and felt whatever we were feeling.

I remember sitting in the courtroom, listening to the prosecutor make her case. She gave the jury an analogy of a bank robber. A bank robber, the prosecutor argued, does not rob every bank, yet, and still, he is a bank robber. Just because Jack did not molest every little girl and family member he came into contact with does not mean he is not a child molester and a predator. Just as a bank robber is a bank robber, Jack Reiss is a molester.

I remember a moment when Jack left the courtroom to go to the restroom. At that same moment I had left the victim office area to go into the courtroom. We were the only two people in the hallway, at opposite ends with about 200 feet between us. When I saw him I clapped my hands. I applauded and congratulated him for his "performance" on the stand. I told him that although he lied out of his teeth, the truth would prevail. I told him he was "going down." meaning he would be convicted for his crimes against humanity.

That year seemed to last an eternity. I fasted often. I would fast completely or, sometimes, I would observe the Daniel fast, a partial fast based on how Daniel, the Old Testament Prophet, would fast only on fruits and vegetables. I somehow felt that fasting could help me get through it all. Keeping my body clear and cleansed somehow helped quiet my mind; it helped me stay connected to my spirit. It somehow made me strong.

On Christmas day 2007, I sent Nikki and Jordan to Maryland to visit their father, Tyrone Sr. He'd been diagnosed with stage 4 cancer, and I knew that it could likely be the last time they would see him alive. I spent that Christmas day home alone and fasted for the last time. As I sat alone in the midst of my final fast, I received the answer I'd been seeking. It came from 2 Samuel 5:20:

"And David came to Baal-perazim, and David defeated them there. And he said, "The LORD has broken through my enemies before me like a breaking flood."

I had read the scripture earlier in the day, yet when I woke up, it flashed before me. At that moment I knew. I knew that the Lord went before me like a flood of waters on my adversary. I knew, sitting there that Christmas day alone and fasting, that our trial— Nikki's and mine and all the children Jack had molested—had already been won!

After that, I gave up my fasting. Although my mind was trying to tell me I needed to fast again, something had changed. I knew I no longer needed to fast. I had no reason to. The victory had taken place in the spirit although we had yet to go to trial. I knew then the battle was over and done. The war I had been waging was spiritual, I just had to wait for the natural manifestation.

A week or two after Jack was convicted, I had the opportunity to see him again; face to face, at his sentencing. They brought him into the court house, along with five or six others, all bound in shackles. He had no idea I was standing there, unseen in a crevice in the hallway. I didn't say anything to him. But for about four seconds, his eyes met mine. He saw me, see him, and that was extremely gratifying. It was what I needed to see. As I watched him shuffle along with his hands and feet chained, I knew he would no longer be able to get to any other little girls.

As I stood there, I prayed that all the young girls he had touched inappropriately would feel the same vindication Nikki and Tamirra were able to feel. I know of a few who did. Another girl Jack had molested, now an adult, called her father after the verdict to say, "We got him, Dad! We got him!"

I was so thrilled to hear that. It filled my heart with triumph, and I knew our victory was a victory for them all. This once, little girl who had lived with the guilt and shame, with the uncertainty and fear, she was now vindicated. Just as though it had been her as a witness on that stand.

Prayer for victory:

Father God in the name of Jesus we come before you the Alpha and the Omega, the Beginning and the End, the First and the Last, the only one True God, we humbly bow before you in submission and triumph. Lord you have gone before us and caused us to be victorious in the battle, and we thank you. Lord it is you and you alone we have looked to and you have shown your mighty hand. Your arm is not to short!

Lord thank you for showing these young girls, they did the right thing by speaking out, by pressing forward, not relenting and because you are not a man that you should lie, you have walked with them as they have pressed through this fiery trial. Now father we ask in the name of Jesus that there be no backlash, that the enemy doesn't come in another door to cause destruction in their lives, and Father, we will forever give you the praise. In Jesus name we pray. Amen.

29. A Time to Heal

(This Is for Your Daughter)

*But unto you that fear my name shall the Sun of righteousness arise with **healing** in his wings;*

Malachi 4:2 (KJV)

I'd like to share with you an experience I had. It was seven years later, and Jack Reiss was in prison. His son was in prison with him for the same offense, believe it or not. Nikki was living in another city, working, going to school, and raising her own little girl.

I was at a prayer service when I recognized that the Lord wanted to heal one of the young ladies there who was dealing with past abuse. I felt the prompting of the Lord for me to step in, to act as this young woman's mother and to let her know that I am the mother of a sexually abused daughter.

In that moment I asked her to see me as her mother. I told her that I had been in that situation and that I was sorry for all she had to go through. I apologized on behalf of her own mother.

I wanted her to feel a mother's love. I wanted her to let me be the mother that hers wasn't. I wanted to tell her how very sorry I was that I was not there for her the way I should have been. In the same way that I put my arms around that young woman that morning, if you are a victim of abuse, let me put my arms around you as you read this.

Let me put my arms around you and tell you that I, as *your* mother, am so very sorry that I didn't recognize the pain in your eyes. I didn't see the signals you were trying to give me to let me know you were hurting.

As I tenderly embraced her and kissed her forehead as only a mother would, let me do the same for you. I planted one kiss after another, intermittently telling her, just as I want to tell you, tenderly and softly, how very sorry I am, how I should have seen and how I should have been there.

I know that, just as this destroyed young woman did at first, you want to draw back from me in disbelief. You want to shrug away from the hurt and from the anger, but this time I refuse to let you go! I am holding you as tight as a mother bear would hold her cub, with all my love, and I WILL NOT let you go until you feel my love.

Then as I continue to kiss you over and over again, to tell you yet again that I'm sorry, that I should have been there for you and that I should have seen, I finally feel you let go of your defenses. I feel the trickle of tears begin to flow down your cheek. I now know that you hear me and you accept that I am right. You know I should have been there for you. You know I should have known. You were just a little girl. It was too much for you to handle. I should have been there.

I'm here for you now; and as it says in Ecclesiastes 4:12, "a threefold cord is not easily broken."

You, I, and the Lord God Jesus Christ can do all things. You are an overcomer. You can and must forgive so that you can live your life without constantly looking backward as you try to go forward.

I want you to feel the love in this apology, and I pray to God that something in you will finally release, that you will finally let go of the hurt and the anger and the shame that has imprisoned you. I pray this book releases you and sets you free.

If you are a mother, I pray you find the strength as a mother to forgive yourself; and if you are a son or daughter, I pray that as a son or daughter you find the strength to forgive your mother for not being there for you, for not protecting you. I am so thankful Nikki so willingly accepted my apology. She, she kept saying, "Mom, you didn't know," but to be honest about it, forgiving myself is and has been the longest step in this journey. While I certainly understand it intellectually, it is still sometimes very difficult to wrap my heart around the fact that I did not know my daughter was being abused in the one place that should have been her haven.

I pray that you release any and all unknown anger you may still, even unwittingly, harbor. Some you can release sooner; some you may release later, but release you must. You are here today, living, breathing and, yes, sometimes crying, because you are a survivor.

Finally, I pray that as the victim of molestation you forgive yourself! You absolutely must forgive yourself because you, as your adult self, expect that as a child you should have been able to stop the abuse. How sad is that? You are blaming a little girl for not stopping an adult from abusing her. Don't do that. Don't do that to yourself! It is imperative to the healing process, for everyone in the circle. Just like a drop of water begins in the center and then it flows outwardly, so too will forgiveness in the family.

I thank God for those who have gone before, those who have suffered *and* shined like Oprah Winfrey, Joyce Meyer, Beth Moore, and Paula White, to name a very few. These inspired women have talked freely about their sexual molestation at the hands of family members, the impact it had on their lives and how God, (once they were in a position to let God reframe the way they looked at things), *ultimately* used their suffering for good. He can and He will do the same thing for you, if you let Him.

The manner in which these strong women of faith have been able to cope with their suffering reminds me of how we played with Silly Putty when we were young. Remember how we would take the Silly Putty and shape it into something? We would stretch it and mold it, conforming it into whatever *we* decided we wanted it to be.

Maybe you have decided that the molestation was the most horrible thing that has ever happened. You feel that it is the most terrible thing that could ever happen to you and that it has ruined the rest of your life forever and ever, amen.

Now, you take that same monstrosity of molestation that you have decided has destroyed your life, and you put it in a beautiful frame and hang it on a wall. You give this beautifully framed horror a place of prominence in your life, and you decide this is what it is—this is what your life is going to look like forever and ever. You see this ugliness on a regular basis, and when anything happens to you, you look at your framed masterpiece, point to it, and say "SEE—I TOLD YOU! MY WHOLE LIFE IS A MESS BECAUSE OF THIS!"

You *can* find another scenario; one in which God walks in. You can take that same lump of Silly Putty, give it to God and say, "God, I don't understand this. I don't know why this happened, but I believe that if anybody can get anything good out of this, YOU CAN. So I'm going to give you this filthy, dirty, nasty lump of clay, and if you can find something good in it, if you can change anything in this that will help someone, if you can show me something positive—well, have at it. I give this to you. It's yours. I no longer want control of this. I'm taking my picture off the wall. I'm taking the monstrosity out of the frame and I want you to reshape and remold it anyway you see fit. Do what you will, Lord. It's okay with me."

Nikki is doing an incredible job at allowing God to reshape the horror of her molestation. She is amazing at what she has accomplished thus far and I marvel. God is good.

Prayer for Healing

Father God, we pray right now for healing for each of our daughters in the name of Jesus. Father, show each of them how to take what happened to them, give it to you, so that you can shape it, reframe it, mold it and do as you please with it. Father, we pray right now in the name of Jesus that the molestation does not become a defining moment in their life that causes them to stop growing and becoming the woman of God that you would have them to be.

She is beautiful, she is special, she is worthy of love and worthwhile. Father, we ask that you go inside and heal all the places that are broken, that are hurt that are bruised, tattered, and torn. You are Jehovah Raphe, you are our healer. Lord, you can heal any situation and anybody; we need you to heal our daughters right now.

This is our prayer, our petition, and our plea; you said we have not because we ask not, Lord, we have come to you today asking and believing that it is your will for her to be healed. In Jesus's name we pray. Amen.

30. More Research Says...

Now, will not God bring about justice for His elect who cry to Him day and night, and will He delay long over them? I tell you that He will bring about justice for them quickly. However, when the Son of Man comes, will He find faith on the earth? Luke 18:7-8 (NASB)

As I continue to try to process, I continue to turn to the statistics. As I struggle to understand, to try to come to terms with the evil that entered my home and tried to destroy my family, I turn to the facts. Somehow knowing the reality helps. Somehow understanding that this is not some vague and unclear evil that has perpetuated itself in our lives makes it, if not easier to accept, easier to look at.

This is a clearly identified evil. It is one that perpetuates itself in our society. It may be a silent crime, as it was for so long for my daughter. But it is a crime, nonetheless, that carries the research and case studies and statistics. It is one that has been studied and reported. And it is one we should all come to understand. Only then can we have a chance to stop it.

More of my research into reports from the Department of Justice revealed this:

- Not all sexually abused children exhibit symptoms—some estimate that up to 40% of sexually abused children are asymptomatic; however, others experience serious and long-standing consequences.
- A common presumption is that children will give one detailed, clear account of abuse. This is not consistent with research; disclosures often unfold gradually and may be presented in a series of hints. Children might imply something has happened to them without directly stating they were sexually abused—they may be testing the reaction to their "hint."

- If they are ready, children may then follow with a larger hint if they think it will be handled well.
- It is easy to miss hints of disclosure of abuse. As a result, a child may not receive the help needed.
- Disclosure of sexual abuse is often delayed; children often avoid telling because they are either afraid of a negative reaction from their parents or of being harmed by the abuser. As such, they often delay disclosure until adulthood.
- Males tend not to report their victimization, which may affect statistics. Some men even feel societal pressure to be proud of early sexual activity, regardless of whether it was unwanted.
- Studies of adults suggest that factors such as the relationship to the perpetrator, age at first incident of abuse, use of physical force, severity of abuse, and demographic variables, such as gender and ethnicity, impact a child's willingness to disclose abuse.
- When children do disclose it is frequently to a friend or a sibling.
- Of all other family members, mothers are most likely to be told. Whether or not a mother might be told will depend on the child's expected response from the mother.
- Few disclose abuse to authorities or professionals.
- Of all professionals, teachers are the most likely to be told.
- Historically, professionals promoted the idea that children frequently report false accounts of abuse. Current research, however, lacks systematic evidence that false allegations are common. Recantations of abuse are also uncommon.

Those who work with sexually abused children know that it is a particularly complicated type of abuse and doesn't even always mean that there has been physical contact. Some abusers like to expose their victims to pornography or other types of sexual situations. Because the children so often know their abuser and

141

believe they should trust him or her, their emotional suffering increases. This is what Jack did to my daughter.

The many ways that children of abuse suffer emotionally are significant and broad. These young victims can feel that they somehow caused their abuse to happen, a guilt that can lead to self-hatred. The resulting shame can also lead to sexual issues when they reach a consenting age. Some have trouble developing intimate relationships; others may become promiscuous.

Many, many young victims of abuse say nothing.

They worry they won't be believed. They worry that it's somehow their fault, and they worry that even if it isn't, that there will be consequences. They find it hard to tell because they are, in a word, afraid. They are afraid of how everyone will react. Will their father want to kill the perpetrator? Will their mother fall apart? Will she even believe their story?

Fearing how others in the family will react—fearing if they will be believed or not-leaves the abused feeling stuck. They feel trapped in a situation over which they have no control.

Children also don't tell because they are ashamed. They feel a huge sense of guilt. They worry others will blame them or be angry with them. If the abuse is within a family, they fear that making their abuse known will destroy their family. They also feel a huge sense of betrayal.

Finally, some children don't tell because a very young child may not understand that what is happening is wrong. They are and will be affected by what is happening, but because they are so young, they have yet to understand the inappropriateness of the behavior.

All of these are reasons so many children do not speak out. And for that reason, children rarely make false accusations. If a child says he or she has been abused, we need to pay attention.

When a child has been sexually abused, there are sometimes warning signals. That, course, is not always the case. But if we are to stand a chance of protecting our children, we need to be aware of the signs:

- A child may have difficulty, because of painful penetration, with walking or with sitting.
- A child might show either interest or understanding of sexual acts or sexual situations that is beyond his or her years.
- Young victims of sexual abuse might begin to avoid a specific person—their abuser—at all costs.
- Children of abuse often refuse to change clothes in front of others, even if it is appropriate such as in front of a parent or at a gym.
- Some children of sexual abuse run away from home in an attempt to end the abuse and escape the horror of their situation.

There are other natural consequences of and normal reactions to the abuse. Some children remain stuck in whatever developmental stage they were in during the early stages of abuse. Nikki was eight-years-old in the early years of her abuse. As the abuse continued, she continued to develop chronologically. She did not develop mentally and emotionally nearly as well.

Children of abuse suffer from shame, from low self-esteem, and from depression. Many become addicted to alcohol and/or drugs. Some find themselves on the streets and enmeshed in a world of prostitution and/or pornography. Others find that they are drawn to the kinds of attention they had—even if they did not enjoy it at the time—and end up either dancing in, working in, or at least spending time in, gentleman's clubs. Most of these children grow up to have at least some issues with trust. It is difficult for them to trust others. Many end up having marital intimacy issues.

When children suffer extremely severe sexual abuse at a very young age, typically during the first three years of life, they can develop what is known as reactive attachment disorder, a condition in which they have trouble forming lasting relationships. They also ultimately lack the ability to have genuine affection for others. Their lives and their emotional coping mechanisms become so detached and chaotic that they cannot establish the normal types of relationships that non-abused children learn to establish.

They may also have great difficulty in reaching the typical milestones of development. Children of abuse who develop reactive attachment disorder need a very special kind of care by experienced professionals.

Prayer for the Little Ones

Father God, in the name of Jesus we come before you right now on behalf of the littlest ones, your children. Lord, you said suffer the little children to come unto me, for such is the Kingdom of Heaven; you told us we had to become like little children, humble and willing to believe. So here we are, Lord, help the littlest, the most vulnerable, the weak, the fatherless, and the preyed on, your children. Father, do it quickly in Jesus's name we pray. Amen.

31. An Evil Across All Bounds

Surely the arm of the Lord is not Too short to save, nor his ear too dull to hear Isaiah 59:1 (NIV)

Child abuse is not something that happens in the ghetto. It doesn't restrain itself to poorer neighborhoods or to those in which the residents are less educated. It doesn't hide away in the darkness—although it takes darkness with it everywhere it goes and leaves its victims in that darkness. If they allow it.

Child abuse affects even the rich and famous. It affects celebrities who seem to have it all, celebrities whom we equate only with the glitz and the glamour of Hollywood. And although these celebrities appear to be on top of the world with their money and looks and talent and power, not all have lived the charmed lives we might think.

Sadly, the horror of child abuse knows no bounds. It reaches its ugly hand out to touch, to defile, any and all. No one is immune. It does not discriminate, but rather can lash out against anyone of us at any socioeconomic level. Even our heroes and movie stars, our favorite artists and professional athletes, are no different than the rest of us when it comes to the threat of child abuse.

It's simply a horror that can seep into any life—however big or small that life appears to be. And because of that truth, recently many celebrities who suffered as children are choosing to step up and talk about their abuse.

As we hear their stories, we begin to understand that they, too, have suffered. They, too, are searching for a way to heal. Paralyzed with the same fear, the same shame that we find so daunting, these celebrities are using the headlines they create to make a difference.

I thank God for that. It has helped me to know that my story is not so unique. It is not only I and it is not only Nikki. It's a story of victimization that many, many others have suffered. It's a story celebrities are beginning to tell thanks to the platform they are fortunate enough to have.

These rich and famous are speaking out as they realize that not only can their stories help others heal, but articulating their stories—talking about what happened to them when they were young—is a way to help themselves heal.

More and more people, celebrities included, are realizing that hiding away in shame only impedes the healing. So rather than feeling trapped and alone, rather than believing there is no help to be had, they are beginning to speak up. They are beginning to tell their stories. And when they do, there are hundreds of thousands of people listening. Hundreds of thousands of young girls and their families can find hope in their stories.

Just as we of the less-famous sort have figured out, when you share your pain, you can minimize it. When others help you understand that pain, the triumph over your pain becomes that much greater.

These are the celebrities that have openly disclosed their sexual abuse:

- Joyce Meyer, Christian Author and Speaker
- Paula White, International Christian Evangelist
- Beth Moore, American Author, Evangelist and Bible
- Oprah Winfrey, Media Personality, Actress, Producer and Philanthropist
- Don Lemmon, CNN Reporter and Anchor
- Tyler Perry, Actor and Entrepreneur
- Donny McClurkin, Minister and Entertainer
- Pamela Anderson, Actress

- Ashley Judd, Actress and Political Activist
- Queen Latifa, Actress and Entertainer
- Antwone Fisher, Writer
- Teri Hatcher, Actress
- Mo'Nique, Entertainer
- Todd Bridges, Child Actor
- Marilyn Manson, Singer
- Tom Arnold, Actor
- Ozzy Osboure, Musician
- Drew Carey, Actor
- Robert Blake, Actor
- Michael Reagan, son of President Ronald Reagan
- Sugar Ray Leonard, Professional Boxer and Olympic Gold Medal Winner
- Scott Brown, Massachusetts Senator
- Cecil Murphy, New York Times bestselling author
- Carlos Santana, Musician
- Chris Brown, Musician
- Cory Haim, Actor
- R. A. Dickey, Professional Baseball Pitcher
- Fiona Apple, Musician
- Rita Hayworth, Actress
- Fran Drescher, Actress
- Fantasia Barrino, Entertainer
- Tim Roth, Actor
- Maya Angelo, Poet
- Sandra Dee, Actress
- Billy Holiday, Singer
- Scott Weiland, Musician
- Tisha Campbell, Actress
- Gloria Gaynor, Entertainer

Prayer for Those Who Have Already Spoken Out

Father God, in the name of Jesus we come before you, thanking you right now for those who have paved the way and spoken out about their molestation. Father, we thank them for their strength, for their courage, their determination; we thank them for no longer holding onto baggage that was never theirs in the first place.

Father, truly they have been examples for so many others, and we ask a special blessing on their lives right now in the name of Jesus. This evil of molestation knows no boundaries, no color barriers, and no financial barriers. It does not care, and it simply wants to leave hurt, heartache, and devastation in its wake. Yet these who have spoken out let it be made known that you can survive, thrive, and fulfill your destiny despite the odds. Thank you for this. In Jesus's name we pray. Amen.

32. Predators Lie in Wait,
But Still a Child Doesn't Tell

Let us not become weary in doing good, for at the proper time we will reap a harvest if we do not give up. Galatians 6:9 (ESV)

"My child would tell me." This is the lie mothers tell themselves. This is the myth with which they live. This is what the soccer moms who car pool their children to the soccer field on Saturdays think. This is what the moms who take their children to gymnastics, the moms who shuttle theirs and the neighborhood kids to the local boys and girls club think. This is what the moms who load the kids up into their minivans to be dropped off at the football games think.

This is what all the moms who are going about their lives and the lives of their children, taking part in the untold number of activities their children participate in, think. As we entrust other adults to care for, protect, and love our children, this is what we think. "My child would tell me."

The truth is that the majority of children, eventually do tell. However, we know that there are far too many predators out there waiting to take advantage of the least likely in our society to have a voice. They take advantage of our little ones, preying on them, hunting them down just as a vulture does a dead skunk in the road, waiting for the opportune time to strike.

These hunters, these stalkers, prey on our children, using their position of authority to silence their victims. They are dad or stepfather or uncle or grandfather. They are coach or priest or teacher. They are there, in the background, waiting until no one else is around, waiting until they have our child by themselves and then like a snake, they strike.

150

When they do strike, they leave a child in a daze wondering what just took place, wondering, "What did H do that made him do that to *me*?" The predators have attacked, leaving behind a venom of shame and fear and guilt; the three terrible things that shuts our children down, that prevents them from talking, that silences them from telling about the horror they have endured.

Yet, we, as mothers, continue to live in our own fantasy. We believe that because we have a fantastic relationship with our children they would tell us. They would tell us if anyone did anything bad to them. NOT SO, MOTHERS. NOT SO, FATHERS. The research tells us that children simply *do not tell* they remain silent for a variety of reasons.

My daughter, Nikki, chose not to disclose her abuse to me for many years, but she is just one among so many. Her reasons for remaining silent for so long may not be your daughter's reasons. The victims of abuse have a myriad of reasons for not speaking up. What you and I and all of society need to know, to understand, to keep in mind and to deal with is that CHILDREN DO NOT TELL or they TELL in their own ways, ways which are not direct.

We need to understand that most abuse is not discovered while it is actively going on. It is not discovered until after the fact. We question how this could happen. How could our children continue to remain quiet? Part of the answer is this:

Have you seen what often happens to those children that come forward and speak up? They are often judged. They are criticized as if somehow the abuse is their fault.

What has your child overheard you say about families who suffer from abuse? What have you said about the child? About the mother? About the family? Were *you* supportive? Or were you accusatory? Were you full of suspicion and doubt? Or were you open-minded, supportive, and ready to lend a hand?

151

Did you quietly put the child on trial? Would you, as a child in this great big, grown-up world, want to walk into the unknown and take a chance? Would you risk asking if someone could or would change things for you? Would you see if your upside-down world could be put right-side up? Could you count on the adults in your world to be open-minded, supportive, and ready to help?

What has been the experience of the few girls that do tell? Their names are dragged through the mud. They are called liars, storytellers, and fabricators. They are told they "misunderstood" the hugs and touches of dear, old grandpa, uncle, coach, dad, stepfather, youth pastor, teacher, leader, insert title-of-authority here. He is a "good guy" and loves kids.

These girls are ostracized. They are talked about everywhere by everybody—in their schools by students up and down the hallways. They are pointed at and whispered about by teachers, staff and administrators. They are pointed at and whispered about in the community, in grocery stores, in convenience stores, in malls and, yes, even in the churches.

These girls are put in the position of proving their abuse. They are told to prove what is done in the dark, in secret. That which is done *intentionally* away from the eyes of anyone must now be proven in order for it to be believed.

I remember in Nikki's pre-trial hearing the defense lawyer recounting the number of windows there were in our home, as if that meant anything. His implication was that surely someone would have *seen* something! To that my response should have been, "And how many times have you been intimate with your wife in your home? How many windows do you have in your home? Surely someone would have *seen* something! GET REAL!"

What else have these few girls who've spoken up had to endure? When they come forward, they walk around with a big scarlet letter "S" for Shame. It is written on their faces and on their bodies. They

152

carry a great big "S" with them everywhere they go. Yes, it may very well be invisible to you, yet it's visible to them. It is visible to the people in their communities as they are whispered about, as they are shunned. They walk around feeling less than human, naked before the world with nothing but a great big "S." They *become* shame. They wear it around there neck like a scarlet letter from the days of the Salem witch trials.

These girls no longer have an identity. They walk around no longer wanting to be who they were. They feel exposed. Their secret is out. Everyone knows what happened to them, and they no longer can wear the façade of being like everybody else. That's because everybody else is not being sexually used by an adult.

They get blamed for what took place when they are finally believed. That's right. In some instances the victims are blamed for what happened to them. If you weren't so fill-in-the-blank, I wouldn't have to treat you/beat you/yell/shout/curse/kick/abuse you - all the excuses people use for not being responsible for their own actions.

During slavery it's what the masters would say before they whipped the slaves into submission.

Mothers would be wise to recognize when they are being abused themselves—not just physically, but emotionally. As a mother you can become paralyzed. Suffering from your own physical and/or emotional abuse can stop you from acting on behalf of your child. It can cause your child to see you as helpless, and, therefore, in her mind, she'll question the point in telling you when you can't even help yourself.

Prayer for Education/Information

Father God, in the name of Jesus we come before you in awe of who you are in our lives. We thank you, Father, for how you have kept us. We thank you for how you are walking us through this difficult time.

Now, Father, we ask right now that your people's eyes are open and in tune to what is truly happening in the world. Lord, give us ears to hear, eyes to see, and a heart to be open to what needs to happen so this information can be disseminated and your people can be educated and stop this scourge on the earth.

Father, use us as instruments in this education, let us not be ashamed to tell someone; we must hold our heads up high so that other parents are more aware and alert. Our nation's children are worth it. Your children are worth it. We can no longer hide in secret silence that is the devil's playground. We must speak up and speak out. In the name of Jesus, this is our prayer. Amen.

33. What Can You Do?

He will wipe all tears from their eyes, and there will be no more death, suffering, crying, or pain. These things of the past are gone forever. Revelation 21:4 (CEV)

The research doesn't lie. Our daughters have a one in four chance of being molested before they turn eighteen. Our sons, one in six. It's shocking. It's disgusting. It's frightening, and it's very, very real. So you *have* to be aware. There is nothing else that will protect our children. Only our vigilance can save them, and sometimes that's not enough.

I was always there for my children. I paid attention. I loved them and nurtured them and did everything a good mom does, and still my daughter suffered abuse at the hands of a monster. But the fact that it happens so frequently mustn't restrain us from trying to stop it.

If your child discloses abuse, the most important thing you can do, and I must repeat this again and again, is to talk. It is also so very important to listen.

Continue to spend time talking to your child. You will probably have to listen very patiently, because many children disclose gradually. After all, most children who have been sexually abused have been hiding their secret away for quite some time. They have been afraid to tell. And although you are as supportive as you know how to be, it will take time for them to find the strength to bring forth all the details of what happened to them.

Talk to your child about any and everything. Let your child know you are not afraid to discuss sensitive subjects. Don't prod too much, and don't get too graphic. It's up to your child to tell her story in the words she chooses; and what can you do other than to talk and to listen?

There are ways to try to protect your child from suffering at the hands of an abuser in the first place. Of course there are no guarantees. There were no guarantees for me. But that doesn't mean you shouldn't try. In fact, if we are ever to remove this scourge from our society, we must all try.

Let your child know that no matter how busy you are, no matter what's going on in your life, if she needs to talk with you, you will *make* time for her. Too often our children see us with our busy lives, and they wonder where they fit in. Don't let someone else make your child feel special. Don't let someone else pick up on your child's emotional needs. YOU be the one to fill the void.

Talk with your child in "other" terms. Give her an opening to discuss what is happening in her life: "I know someone else is dealing with (you pick the topic). Have you ever felt that way?" Or "I remember when I was going through a rough stage…" Giving our children openings, giving them little prompts, provides them a chance to broach topics they might not otherwise broach. It gives them an opportunity to say, "Yes. I'm struggling. I'm having trouble, and I could use your help."

It's also really important to let your child know you are human. You are not perfect. Sometimes our kids believe that we as parents are above any hurt or confusion or shame or conflict. If you can be someone they can touch, if you can show your child your flaws and, yes, even your scars, she will be far more likely to open up to you.

When you speak to your child from a place of love rather than from a place of fear, your child will feel that love and respond with trust. If you try to have a conversation about either real or suspected abuse and all the while you are dealing with a rising panic within yourself, your child will pick up on your concern. She'll be far less likely to confirm your fears. She will not want to cause you further stress. Having a calm and casual demeanor and tone is essential.

We really should begin these conversations with our children when they are very young. We must have them naturally and regularly. Of course you don't want to hound your children and make them afraid of their very shadows. But having a conversation about their rights and their privacy is essential—even when they are very young and only beginning to understand it all. They will learn that having absolute control over their own bodies is a true and natural fact of life. They will come to understand that if someone is hurting them, they have every right and reason to tell them to stop and to tell us what is happening.

Consider this: We teach our children not to run out into the street. We love them and we want them to be safe. Just as we train them when they are very young, without causing undue fear, not to cross the street because it's dangerous, we can teach them that someone might try to sexually abuse them.

Yes, the words may seem awkward and strange to use with your young child. But again, I say that we MUST do all that we can. Teaching your child about her body and her rights and the dangers of abuse does not mean it will happen. In fact, it could mean that it won't.

As your child gets a little older and the conversation becomes more natural, help her know that she should trust her instincts. If she feels that the attention of someone isn't quite right, he needs to know that he can and should speak up. This is so important because we aren't always around. We don't know who the predators are. It is a sad fact that many of these predators are people that we, as parents, trust.

If a child knows absolutely that she can and should trust her "gut," then perhaps she can stop an abuse perpetuated by someone whom we would never, in our wildest of dreams, imagine could do such a thing to our child.

We must be absolutely sure to tell our children that *we will believe them*. They will not be in trouble. We will take them seriously. Tell your child that an abuser will say and do *anything* to keep the abuse a secret. Your child must know that he can and should speak up.

Most importantly of all, remember that these conversations need to continue. Have them openly and casually and regularly. We tell our children repeatedly—in a non-threatening way—to be very, very careful when they cross the street. We need to tell them repeatedly—in a non-threatening way—to be very, very aware of sexual predators.

Prayer for Communication

Father God, in the name of Jesus we come before you today, asking you to help us talk to our children about areas that are not always easy for us to talk about. Teach us, Father, how to bring up topics, how to speak to our children without our emotions; give us courage, Father.

The lack of communication creates miscommunication and understanding...there's been enough of that already, Father. I will face my fears, and yes, I will even learn to say "I don't know" to my daughter. Father, there is no time like the present, and I know she needs me know more than ever. There is nothing that will be off limits in our conversations. I can do all things through Christ who strengthens me, in Jesus's name I pray. Amen.

34. Charlie's Angels

A friend loveth at all times, and a brother is born for adversity.
Proverbs 17:17 (KJV)

Nikki and her two friends, Nancy and Carissa: one black, one white, one a combination of both—all lovely, all beautiful. With one on either side of Nikki, they supported her, they were her friends, they were there when she had to go to court for the first time. They were there at the pretrial when she had to speak. They were there to hear what her stepfather had been doing to her since she was a little girl.

The legal process is a twisted tale of ups and downs and of lawyers' maneuverings. Our lawyers worked to try to "out plan" the opposition, and, *yes*, Jack Reiss and his lawyers were the opposition. They were the enemy. Sides were taken.

Only this time, the opposition was not just the perpetrator of the crime. Our opposition included his entire family, his extended family, and friends and associates. Our opposition included anyone he could bring into his web and whisper to them of my evil intent and of his virtue. There was always a hint of "Another Somebody Done Somebody Wrong Song" playing in the background.

Manipulative personalities contrive in every situation to show how THEY were simply trying to help someone but THEY were injured in the process. Manipulative personalities dominated our opposition.

You, too, may have to experience this. You may confront the fact that you are not just dealing with the molestation itself, but with all that goes along with it. This type of violation is not the kind that is committed in the open; it's not the kind people readily talk about. It's like a death that no one wants to speak of. Yet for you and for your family and for your victimized child, a death has occurred, however unspoken it may be. All of you will need to find ways to cope with the shattered pieces and fragments that are left behind.

A Prayer for Friends

Father God, in the name of Jesus we come to you for no other reason other than to say thank you. Thank you, Father, for being a friend to us and for giving friends who have stood by us during this season of our life and our daughter's life. Father, had it not been for friends, we would not have been able to weather this storm. We will forever be grateful to our friends. So, Father, we ask that you bless our friends in an abundance. Bless them with your love, with your grace, with your mercy. Bless them in their coming out and their going in. Bless the fruit of their body, Father; bless their finances, bless their relationships, bless their marriages, bless their children, their children's children, and bless them real good, Father. We thank you, Father, for friends who are with us through the good and the bad. We thank you that you didn't give us fair-weather friends! This is our prayer in Jesus's name. Amen.

35. Restoration

And after you have suffered a little while, the God of all grace, who has called you to his eternal glory in Christ, will himself restore, confirm, strengthen, and establish you.

1 Peter 5:10 (ESV)

This is the ultimate goal. Restoration means to restore back to its original condition. It means a return to normal and healthy. That is the promise the Lord gives to us when we submit our lives to him and trust Him throughout the process. He promises us restoration. He promises to make us whole.

I have witnessed His transformative work in my life. I've seen His work in my daughter's life, in my family's lives, and in the lives of my extended family. I have watched Him work to restore the lives of my friends, my church family, and my community. To this day, I still see how the Lord is working to restore, how He is working to heal, Jack's family.

Understand that this entire ordeal has been very difficult for Jack's family as well. They have suffered. They have had pain. No one wants to hear that their family member is a child molester. The words create shock. They elicit utter disbelief. They cause tremendous anger. Someone they love, a member of their very own family, has been accused of a hideous crime. But it happens. It did happen. Their family member was not only accused, he was tried, found guilty and convicted. They could not pretend it hadn't happened. He did it.

Jack's family is not alone in their shock and disbelief. They are not alone in standing by and having to watch a family member tried, convicted, and sentenced for such a horrific crime. Others have gone before and, sadly, others will follow. Ninety percent of all molestation is committed by family members and friends. It is not perpetuated by strangers.

I continue to pray for the restoration of Jack Reiss's family. I pray for all the families that must come to terms with the fact that one of their own—one of their family members whom they have loved and trusted—is a child molester. I pray that they, too, will find a way to deal with the shame and the guilt. I pray that they, too, can find some kind of answers to the endless questions: What did we miss? Why didn't we see something? How could we not have known?

Perhaps, in the end, it's the unanswered questions that haunt a family the most: Did he molest any of our children? Would our children tell us if he did? Or did we blindly trust him because he is a relative, not knowing that our trust was so totally, so completely, misplaced?

All of us who have been affected by the horror of molestation-live with these haunting questions. Over and over and over again, we ask: Why do molesters molest? Why do pedophiles do what they do?

Even as I question, I pray. I pray for the restoration of the abusers. I want to see them returned to their original state. I sincerely ask God to restore them to a healthy and normal condition. I do not want to see another child hurt. I do not want to see any more of our precious babies abused or traumatized. The cost is just too great.

Anna Salter, a psychologist and author, wrote an eye-opening book about sexual predators: "Predators: Pedophiles, Rapists and Other Sex Offenders," attempting to answer some of the questions: What is their motivation? Why do they do this? Why do so few get caught?

Salter frames her analysis around stories of the abusers, explaining that sexual molesters are highly sophisticated in the ways they deceive. She highlights how they manipulate, using the misconceptions, misunderstandings, and misinterpretations of those who might, but so often do not, discover what they are doing. This is how they get away with it. This is how they avoid getting caught. Salter argues that even the most intuitive of us can be fooled by their deceitful performances. She works and she writes to try to help us understand, to try to provide us the tools we need to protect our children.

It is an amazing book. Get it. Read it. It will open your eyes. Her writing explains that some molesters commit this heinous crime for the thrill they get from being manipulative. They find intense pleasure in the game of it all. They plan to do it again and again, all for the intoxicating enjoyment they receive from getting away with it. And those of us who are their victims continue to be manipulated. We continue to trust, especially in the Christian community where we both want and need to be forgiving. What we sometimes are, however, is naïve and gullible, leaving our children vulnerable to these monsters who prey on them.

Do I believe if Jack were released today that he would stop molesting children? As a Christian, I believe all things are possible with God. That being said, however, I would not have *any* child within five miles of him. Ever.

Jack Reiss did not wait until he was in his forties to become a molester. He had other victims. Perhaps he had many. And because he was able to get away with his crimes for so long, he became bolder. He continued his obsession, which is what molesting becomes to an abuser. He continued and grew more daring, attacking more and more victims, until he thought himself invincible.

What Jack did not realize was that he had finally met his match. He did not realize that he had run up against a meek, mild-mannered, sweet little girl, who is the person I initially was, who would eventually bring him down. I was the meek and quiet woman who he thought he could bully and intimidate. He was convinced that I would cower down. He thought he could control me with his rantings and his rage, and for a long, long time he did. But, eventually, I began to stand up. When I had finally had enough of his immature, kindergarten behavior, I got a backbone and did what needed to be done. I got that crazy man out of my house; and that is what gave Nikki the freedom to tell me what she hadn't told me before. Praise God.

Prayer for Restoration

Our Father and our God, glory to your name. Father, we your daughters come before you asking right now that you would restore everything the enemy stole from us. We ask in the mighty name of Jesus that you restore our health, lost finances, lost love, restore our daughters to their former selves, Lord, any and everything that the enemy touched, we reclaim and purify it right now in the name of Jesus.

We reclaim any and everything the enemy thought he had stolen from us, Father, in the name of Jesus. Father, you said to declare a thing, so we declare right now that we are whole, we are well, healthy, we are sound, we are secure in who we are. Our hearts are pure, our motives are pure, our family is secure, our daughter is well, our mind, our emotions are whole, bound, assured, no longer seeping and leaking the issues of life.

Lord, we are restored, reestablished, returned in every area of our life; our children are well, our husbands are well, our friends, our church family, every area of our lives that was touched by this fiery trial will prosper as they see us come out like pure gold, leaning and depending on you and you alone. And it is so in Jesus's name. Amen

36. A Thousand Pieces

For I reckon that the sufferings of this present time are not worthy to be compared with the glory which shall be revealed in us. Romans 8:18 (NIV)

I had Nikki in counseling. I had begun the process of seeking justice so that her perpetrator could not go out and repeat the harm he's caused on another little girl. But I was sinking farther and farther into my own dark hole. I reached out to my friends, and their reaction was one of concern that I was about to lose it, which I was, yet it was as if that were not acceptable. It is perfectly all right for the victim to fall apart. It is not all right for the mother of the victim.

So here I was and am, completely traumatized and alone in so many ways. And the questions circled unanswered in my head.

Where do I go? To whom do I turn? Who can possibly relate to what I am feeling? I have to be strong for my daughter. I cannot let her see me falling to pieces. I have to be strong for my son. I am still a mother with two children to raise and support. I have to be strong for my mother, who just lost her husband and is in need of a great deal of support. I have to be strong in my community and in my church as a leader.

Yet here I am with this hole in my soul. I have been kicked in the teeth, my heart has been dragged through the mud and my daughter has been abused, but I can't even fall apart!

What I really want to do was to go somewhere and pull my hair out. I want to scratch my skin off and pluck out my teeth. I wanted to go into an insane asylum and bounce off the walls and scream until there's nothing left on the inside.

Yet I didn't get the opportunity to fall apart. Like so many people who are in the spotlight—although I am by no means purporting I am in their category, I understand how they must feel in terms of not being able to live a normal life—I do not get an opportunity to scream and run and fall apart.

My daughter has been molested and this bastard did it!

How do you get that back? How do you undo it? How do you unring a bell that has already rung! How do you get back words that have already been spoken and are out there in the atmosphere?

I so wanted to bargain with God. I so wanted to turn back the hands of time and switch places with my daughter. I so wanted to change one or two courses of our life so that this had not happened. I wanted Samantha of *Bewitched* to twitch her nose so that we could go back in time. I wanted one more chance to change the course our lives had taken.

Before I married Jack Reiss, I had asked God clearly to tell me if there were any reason that I should not marry him. He didn't. WHY? WHY? WHY? Now that question ruminated in my mind like a broken record I couldn't get off the track no matter how hard I tried.

Yet through this entire ordeal I pretended to go about my day. I dutifully smiled. I did my normal duties. I cooked and took my children here and there. You can believe, though, that Lisa the person was in NONE of it.

I sent my body to do what must be done. My spirit and soul were no longer attached or a part of me. They had taken leave. Somewhere off and distant, my heart and soul were on a search for answers that only God could provide. They were on a search for a peace that only God could bring.

Prayer for Reconciliation

Father God, in the name of Jesus, we your daughters, who are mothers, but right now we need to be mothered, come to you our creator, our soft place to land, and ask you to gather us back together as we are so scattered right now. Father, reconcile us to ourselves. Father, we are torn apart, and our parts have been tossed in the wind.

Father, we don't know where to begin to pick up the pieces of our soul and spirit. The work that needs to be done in us can only be correctly done by the one who made us, and that is you. So, Father, here we are naked before you, no longer trying to put up a front, no longer in need of being anything to anyone else until you touch us and pick up the fragments of our tattered soul. We cry unto you, our God and our king.

We cry out, "It's me, it's me, O Lord, standing in the need of prayer, not my father, not my sister, but it's me, O Lord, standing in the need of prayer." I know now what I never knew before, Lord, I know what it is to be so low you are the ground. Yet I can say like Job said, I know that my Redeemer lives, and because you live, Lord, you are my hope, you are my joy, you are my salvation, you are my reason to go own; Lord, I know that with you I can do all things through Jesus Christ my Lord and Savior. This is our prayer, this is our plea, you are an ever-present help in this our time of need. Amen.

37. Pieces Re-sewn

To appoint unto them that mourn in Zion, to give unto them beauty for ashes, the oil of joy for mourning, the garment of praise for the spirit of heaviness; that they might be called trees of righteousness, the planting of the Lord that he might be glorified. Isaiah 61:3 (KJV)

My recommendation to you is to pick up every fragment that you can and hold on to it. You may not have the energy, the time nor the courage to put the pieces back together at this time, but there will come a time when you will want to reassemble those pieces again.

There will come a time when you will be able to look at those shards and not see them solely as fragments. You will come to see the beauty in them as they are, and you will know that almighty God in his infinite wisdom can take those fragments, if you give them to him, and mend them together to bring life out of death. He can breathe on you, on your daughter, and on your family. He can bring new life to your spirit.

Yes, your weary fragmented bones can live again, but not now, not until you're ready, not until you have gone into those deep, dark, lonely, lowly recess of your mind, heart and soul.

Yes, it is hard. Yes, it is lonely. Yes, it is cold. And, yes, you are all alone to deal with it. Or so you think.

I had to write this story. And though it has not been an easy journey, if this book helps one mother survive this horrendous period in her life, it will be worth every tear I cried as I've written. It will be worth the horror of reliving the painful days and nights.

I pray that no one has to experience that loneliness I felt. The sheer and utter disbelief of what my daughter had to suffer nearly drove me insane. And as I searched for a way, anyway, to get through it, I realized there are no resources to help mothers cope with their own feelings—with their own guilt and shame. There are no texts to guide the mothers through the nightmare they must live as they help their daughters cope with abuse.

We as mothers are an island unto ourselves. I don't know why that is. I stopped looking for an answer. I know that our American society does not consider mothers in the equation of abuse in any truly substantive way. This is a reality that must change.

As a mother who has had to find her own ways to cope, I urge our mental health professionals to reach out to these non-offending mothers in a way that has not been done before. They are an underserved population that feels they have no right to speak up for themselves. They feel no right to get help for themselves when it is their daughters or their sons who have been abused.

When you fly on an airplane, you are given safety instructions. Parents, who naturally want to care for their little ones before they care for themselves, are instructed to put their breathing masks on first. Only then should they place a mask on their child. I question what those in the mental health field might learn from this analogy when it comes to caring for the custodial non-offending mother. I wonder what you as the mother of a sexually abused child might learn.

Are you trying to put your child's mask on while you can barely breathe? Are you using all your resources to save your child's life and, thereby, going to lose yours? Have you used all your strength, energy, resources, and any fortitude you might have to get through the day for your child, all to the point that there is nothing left for you?

We cannot continue to do so. And those in the professional world of mental health who might be able to save us must start to speak out. They must tell us to put our masks on first. They must help us understand that only when we can breathe, only when we have the strength of oxygen flowing through our own bodies, can we do anything substantial to help our children.

Perhaps you are everyone's hero but feel like a complete failure on the inside. Perhaps you feel like a fake. Like a caricature or a put-on. If only they knew, you think to yourself, how much you are dying on the inside. If only they knew that you are drowning in midair. If only they knew that you take each step as though you are walking in mud. And yet you continue to push on. You continue to put one foot in front of the other.

Understand that all of these feelings are okay. They are natural. They are expected. Your weeping may endure for a night, because this may be your night to cry. Or not. Perhaps it's your night to moan and to groan. It is your night to do and be whatever you need to do and be. God knows it and He understands.

Know that this is just a season, and just like summer, spring, winter, and fall pass away, so will this. It will not always be like it is right now. It is a season that we need to survive. It is a season in which we must take comfort that God's grace is sufficient to get us through. It is his grace made perfect in our weakness, and if we can only lean on Him, He will save us. If we will only trust our Lord Jesus during this horrible time, He will surely bring us out. We must remember his promise—that without faith it is impossible to please Him. As horribly difficult as it is, we must maintain our faith.

Know also that your daughter is looking to see how *you* handle this. She will take her cues from you. As a loving mother, you have always been an example for her. It is during this crucial time that you are more of an example than you have ever been before. You must be. You must be a model for her. You must show her how to handle such a time of crisis in her life. You must model the type of faith you want her to have.

I pray that you find the strength needed to take this journey. Yes, it is painful. Yes, you will cry. But I know beyond a shadow of a doubt that if you commit to believing when you cannot believe—if you determine to believe anyway—you WILL get to the other side.

You will reach the shore of the other side where there is yet hope, strength, love, and joy. You will reach the shore of the other side where a final fullness of comfort and peace awaits.

I pray that the God of Love fill you to overflowing. I pray that you know that His promise to never leave or forsake you is real. I pray you boldly go to the Throne of Grace where you can find help in this time of need. I pray that you continue on toward the throne, as He never tires of seeing or hearing from you.

Know always that the Lord has told us that we do not have to suffer alone. Know that He has promised our protection. God tells us in Isaiah 43:2 (ESV):

When you pass through the waters, I will be with you; and through the rivers, they shall not overwhelm you; when you walk through fire you shall not be burned, and the flame shall not consume you.

He knows our grief and our pain. He knows our heartache. He has made us a promise that with His help, we will survive.

Prayer for Stability

Father, we pray right now for your daughters, the mothers. Father, we pray that they not waiver from their faith. Father, strengthen them in the inner man that their faith faint not. They will need strength for the journey that is before them; some days will be easier than others, so I ask that you go before them, send your angels to encamp about them and encourage them that yes, they can and will get to the other side.

Father, every battle, every test, every trial is not easy, and this is one of the harder tests in life, but if they will just hold on to your unchanging hand and lean and depend on you daily, if they will tell *you* about their fears, their struggles, if they will bring *you* their tears and their heartaches, Father, you promised that you would see them through. Father, I pray right now that their faith not waiver.

Father, give them a double portion. Let them know that when they are running on empty they can always return to the Rock of their salvation for a refill, because that Rock will never run dry. Father, cause them to know that they can call on you day or night, night or day. Father, let your daughters know they can crawl into their Father's lap anytime, day or night, and feel the warmth of your love and feel the Father's arm holding them.

There will be many days ahead where they need to know no man, no woman, no living breathing person can do what our Heavenly Father can do. The peace that surpasses all understanding will keep your minds and hearts through Christ Jesus. This is a prayer and a promise, in Jesus's name. Amen.

38. Mother and Daughter

Now faith is confidence in what we hope for and assurance about what we do not see. Hebrews 11:1 (NIV)

Nikki and I have an excellent relationship today. We are each other's friend, support, and encouragement. We are each other's cheerleader, and, at times, we are each other's confidant and prayer partner.

Nikki knows she can talk with me about anything at any time. She knows she can call whenever she needs me. She knows she can confide in me. Now, as a twenty-four-year-old single mother herself, she knows she can be "real" with me. She doesn't have to hide anything or pretend that she's okay when she may not be.

She knows that I love her, and that I have some understanding of her struggles. More than anything else, though, she knows I want to see her happy. She knows that I want to see her successful and well-established. She knows I want her to be able to care for her six-year-old daughter, Charis.

You see, Nikki knows that when the rubber hits the road, I will always be her mother *and* her friend. My love for her is a never-ending circle, one through which we continually go in and out. Together we weave in and out, according to what is necessary in the moment. When her need is for a mother, I can be her mother. When her need is for a prayer partner, I can be her prayer partner. When her need is for a girlfriend, I can be her girlfriend. If her need is for a listening ear, I am there to listen to anything and everything she has to say. When she just wants to share a funny story, I am there to listen and to laugh.

Together we mourn for her grandmother—my mother—who recently and unexpectedly passed away. She had always been a part of our lives, of everything Nikki and I did, whether she was physically present or not. So when Nikki is sad, or when something happens, which it often does, that reminds her of her grandmother and she simply needs someone to understand, she knows I am here for her. Losing that lovely woman who had always been a part of our lives has been very difficult for both of us. No longer are we three generations of strong women. Now we are only two.

But Nikki and I carry on and continue to be two strong women who stand together. Recently she sent me a picture of herself just to say… "I look like you." We both had to laugh. I said, "Yes, you do!"

The strength of our bond comes from all that we've been through together: not just the horror of the abuse, but all the good times that came before and all the good times that have come after.

We've have always had such fun together. We went on a Caribbean cruise together with the family and had the time of our lives. We do simple things together as well. We go shopping. We do things with Charis, Nikki's daughter—my precious little grandbaby. We took Charis to Disneyworld for her fifth birthday. Charis absolutely loved it and is, of course, ready to go back. That was such a fun trip, and I am blessed that we can make those wonderful memories. I am blessed that we will have those wonderful memories forever to share.

Together, as mother and daughter, Nikki and I have gone to counseling. We have put in the time and the effort needed to work through some of the issues that we've had to confront—both individually and together. As a result of all that we have been through and all we did to survive, we are stronger.

I thank God for my daughter. I thank God that she respects me, and I praise God that I can respect the woman that she is. I love my daughter so very much and I know that she loves me.

I absolutely cherish who Nikki is right now—who she is today. She is like a many-faceted jewel that, when you hold it up to the light, it shines. It sparkles at so many different angles.

I have every expectation that although she had a very difficult period in her life, it was NOT the defining moment for her. It was not the be-all and end-all of who she would become. It was not the final chapter of her life. She has grown and adapted so well that I happily cannot even say it was a pivotal time of her life around which everything else revolved. Rather, it was a difficult period that she came through. She came out the other side with wisdom and with strength.

Each and every day I thank God that He did not let her life end with the molestation she experienced at such a young age.

Did she fall into some of the known traps that the research say can ensnare victims, especially child victims, of abuse? Yes, she did. As so many of the statistics report, she become a single, teenaged mother. But that has not stopped her.

Thankfully, Nikki is a bright and mature young woman. She knows the pitfalls of having suffered abuse. She recognizes the challenges before her. She is strong and insightful and has worked through some things she's needed to work through. I am so very proud to say she went to college and is currently pursuing her nursing degree. My Nikki is a born nurturer. She is an excellent mother to Charis and will be an excellent nurse. I'm very, very proud of the young woman she is.

I now view what we went through and how we went through it as an example for other mothers and daughters, or any children and parents, who have to go through this painful trial. Today I can truly see our experience as a beacon of hope for others who must suffer in the same way we did. I see it as proof that you—all of you—can come out on the other side. You can come out better—healthier and stronger and more resilient. When you decide to stick together as a family, when you decide to fight—and I mean really, really FIGHT—for your sanity, for your health and for your wholeness, you can and will triumph. You can and will be whole again.

Prayer for Relationships

Our Father and our God, we come before you, as your daughters. Father, we come before you as your children, we come before you with bowed down head and humbled hearts asking on behalf of mothers and daughters everywhere that you bless relationships, Father, and bless them abundantly. Father, cause mothers and daughters to love one another like never before; cause mothers and daughters to communicate with each other, to feel for each other, to see into each other to have an abiding respect for each other, to be each other's encourager, to be each other's cheerleader, to be each other's friend.

O God, I ask that you bless, that the blood of Jesus would protect the mother and daughter bond, Father, let them be like Ruth and Naomi in the Bible where there was always an abiding respect, a love that was pure and that was God given. Father this is our prayer in Jesus's name we pray. Amen.

39. Finally

For the eyes of the LORD move to and fro throughout the earth that He may strongly support those whose heart is completely His. 2 Chronicles 16:9 (NASB)

I want to share with you the words of my daughter. They are so important. They are a way for you to see her standing on the other side of what she went through. And that is exactly where she is today. She went through a horrible, horrible period in her life, and she survived. Together we managed. Together we came out on the other side.

I asked Nikki to write something to the mothers. I asked her to write something for *you*. I want for you to hear her words. I can tell my story. I can reach out to the Moms who are suffering this unbearable hurt and tell them what happened to us and how we managed to survive it. I can give guidance and make suggestions. I can tell them how important it is that they simply *be there* for their child once that child has disclosed.

But until they/you hear my daughter's voice, the voice of the once-little girl and now-grown-woman, they/you cannot know the truth of what I'm saying.

Until you hear my daughter say how important it was and is that a mother stand strong by her child, you cannot fully feel the impact.

I love my daughter. Even as she tells me that she is proud of me, I am so very proud of her. The next chapter is what she wrote:

40. Nikki's Message to All Mothers

I'm so proud of you. You were my voice when I couldn't speak, my protection when I couldn't fight, and my comfort when I was so lonely. I know you think that you failed me, but you could never be more wrong. I felt like everything in life wasn't worth living until you showed me that there can be beauty in ugly situations. I can't thank you enough, even though sometimes it may be hard.

I want to start off by saying IT'S NOT YOUR FAULT.

When I was a little girl, you told me to watch out for certain things even though I couldn't see the danger in them. You knew there would be tremendous battles that I would have to fight, so you prayed over me day and night. God heard and answered all those prayers.

I know this to be true because I am untainted by a battle the devil thought he won. I may not be exactly where I want to be quite yet, but with your help and the grace of the Lord, day by day, we're going to get there! Did I mention how much I love you? I know I couldn't have asked for a better mother. To see my Mom be as strong as an ox and as soft as a feather to support me in this difficult time was and is amazing.

If there was any doubt in my mind that God wasn't real (and there was plenty), you solidified His presence. Today, I'm absolutely positive that His love is pouring through you into me. What an example you are! You are the true definition of WOMAN with such couth. You are cultured and refined. You are so strong.

One of the best lessons you've taught me in all this is how to take such an awful, nasty, embarrassing situation and still walk around with my chin high and my crown in place because I'm still the princess you've always said I am. I'm not sure everybody could handle such a life-altering state as that which you and I are in. But

God appointed you and me to do this, so I'm going to grab your hand and walk this thing out. Sometimes I may squeeze tighter and other times I might let go, but just know that WE can do this. There will be plenty of time later for yelling and arguing about things that don't matter, but today and always, it's me and you.

This will take our relationship to new lengths I never knew were possible, and, believe it or not, I love every bit of it. I just want you to know I love you. I adore you, and when I grow up, if I could have one-third of your beauty, poise, strength, diligence, wisdom, knowledge and love, I would be the happiest woman in the world. With everything going on, sometimes I might get caught up in it all and forget to tell you. I might even push those feelings to the back burner so I have some room to deal with it all. But just know I love you. You mean the world to me.

I am so proud of you for having the courage to write this book to help other mothers that have experienced this. I support you 100 percent and want all the mothers to get encouragement from our experience.

Thank you for seeing my hurt and helping me with all this pain. Now that I'm a mother, I'm going to pray over my little girl just as you showed me when you prayed over me. I'm going to reveal to her the love and strength that God can give us in any and all situations.

Thanks, Mom,

Nikki

41. Life After the Storm

You will forget your misery; you will remember it as waters that have passed away. Job 11:16 ESV

I have written this book as difficult as it has been out of an act of obedience, love, faith and trust in my Redeemer. It is not easy being open and transparent, yet I know it to be necessary and I'm honored that he would trust me with this very important task.

For that reason alone is enough, yet there's more, you see even though I know this work is of the Lord I recognize beyond a shadow of a doubt I needed to write this to help others who have gone through what we did, and I want to share my journey with you, whoever you are, so when God told me to. Yes I am one of those "silly" people who believes in a transcendent omnipresent, omniscient, and omnipotent being which created us and interacts with those who seek him.

As a matter of fact, The Lord *required* that I do this. He said this book must be published, and I was being *disobedient* in taking so long to write it. (That's not something you ever want to hear from above. I was a basket case after *that* experience. Why did I have to do it? Because you need to know there is LIFE AFTER THE STORM!

You need to know that weeping endures for a night, but joy comes with the morning (Psalm 30:5). You need to know that you will laugh again, you will love again, and you will live again. You need to know that your daughter also will laugh again; she can and will get back to being herself again. You need to know that in time, your family will be whole again, complete, fulfilled, and lacking nothing!

How can these things be? Not by might. Not by your strength or by my strength. But only by His spirit (Zechariah 4:6). What God did for me, he will surely do for you *if* you let Him. *If* you surrender. *If* you go through it all and vow not to be bitter. If you make up your mind not to let the perpetrator take *anything* else from you and your family, God will *surely* take your life, which may look like ashes right now, and turn those ashes into something of beauty.

There is only one way to win in a no-win situation. You can't undo what has been done. You can't give back those days and nights to your daughter. You can't change what took place in the past, no matter how much you want to.

I SO wanted to change what had happened. LORD knows I did! I would have given my life to change what happened to my daughter, but how could I? How can YOU? I couldn't. Neither can you.

So focus on what you *can do*! You *can* change her future. You see, you really only have two options here. You can be bitter for the rest of your life and let what happened define who you are forever as it seeps into every area of your life and you become an old, nasty, evil, bitter person. You can look at the world from cynical eyes and watch as people slowly stop wanting to be around you because you are mean, spiteful, and cruel.

Or you can put what happened into its proper context. You can make the choice to forgive so that you do not drink the poison of unforgiveness, a poison which torments your own spirit. You can ask God to heal all the broken places in your heart, in your daughter's heart and in your family.

You can ask God to give you a greater capacity to trust Him when you feel yourself weak and faltering.

Then you can go and sit by the rivers of water in Psalm 1:1 (ESV): "Blessed is the man that walks not in the counsel of the wicked." nor stands in the way of sinners–you can mosey on down to Psalm 27 and wait and let Him strengthen your heart. You can get up and taste and see that the Lord is good over in Psalm 34. Then you can go and get washed from all your iniquity at Psalm 51.

After you've washed for a while, you can go over to Psalm 2 and talk to God about those who are waiting to see your demise. Then you can head straight up to Psalm 24. Do not stop for any reason, for the earth is the Lord's and the fullness thereof…lift up your heads, O gates! And be lifted up, O ancient doors that the King of glory may come in. Who is this King of glory? The Lord of hosts, he is the King of glory! Selah (Psalm 24:1, 7-8, ESV).

Abiding Prayer

Now may the God of Heaven, and his Son Jesus the Christ, Bless you and keep you, may he forever keep you in perfect peace as you keep your eyes stayed on him, Lord we will not focus on what you see in the natural, as we know this is only temporary, we will remember to walk by faith and not by sight, for without faith it is impossible to please you. This is a faith and an endurance walk on this earth, and we live in a fallen earth, an earth full of sin that entered with Adam and Eve, with that Father let us remember that we are in this world and not of this world.

Do not let us get consumed with the things of this world. Lord we declare and decree that our sons and daughters will not succumb to death, hell and destruction at the hands of the enemy but because you came to give life and life more abundantly, our children shall live and not die and declare the works of the Lord, the goodness of the Lord, the faithfulness of the Lord, through every trial, through every hard time, they will not give up, they will not give in, they shall come through it like pure gold and we your representatives on this earth shall lean, depend, and trust in you and you alone. In Jesus name we pray. Amen. And it IS SO!

You Will Survive

More than anything else I want you to know that you can survive through this. It is imperative that you know this. You will survive, your daughter will survive, and with your help, support, encouragement, and faith she can thrive into the person the Lord meant for her to be.

Just know that while this may be one of the more difficult periods in your life, you must press in and rely on your faith, your family, and friends, know that our Lord's promises are true! "He'll never leave you nor forsake you" Deuteronomy 31:8. "Lo I am with you always, even unto the end of the world." Matthew 28:20

Make the scriptures personal to your situation, to your struggle to where you are in that moment, that hour, or that day. You must use every spiritual weapon you have in your arsenal, fast often, pray without ceasing, plead the blood of Jesus over your daughters, heart, her future, her destiny in Christ, cry loud unto him who is our Comforter, that's why he said "Come unto me, all who labor and are heavy laden..." Matthew 11: 28 don't stop coming to him, he never tires of hearing from you. Bring every concern, every heartache, every issue before the Father, and encourage yourself with Psalms, hymns, and songs that are uplifting.

Let your daughter see you believe with her and in her as she continues to blossom and grow. Be certain that this is just a season, and just like summer, fall, winter and spring, if you continue to take one step at a time, lift your head, lift your daughters head, hold on to each other through the process, give each other space when needed, but know she is looking to you for her direction, you make a world of difference in her life.

To you, I say "Hold your head up high, you have nothing to be ashamed of!"

This is not the time to be around negative people, and make sure you don't become negative yourself! Listen to yourself, what you say and how you sound when you are talking...ensure everything that comes out of your mouth does not have a negative bent to it.

Every day, week, month and year you will see the progress being made to the ultimate goal, and I promise you, if you make the decision to trust God through this, you will look back and give him all the praise, all the honor and all the Glory, you will be absolutely amazed at how far you, your daughter, indeed the entire family has come as you lean in and lean on his everlasting arms.

I'm a living testament to what the Lord will do. Trust him will all your heart, your mind, and when you are overwhelmed---trust him anyhow! Every time the devil came to torment me in my mind, I found myself saying this over and over and over again---Lord I trust YOU! Lord I trust YOU! Lord I trust YOU! I would say it five, ten, sometimes twenty times until I felt the relief and release in my spirit. I would say it openly, sometimes I said it in my mind, but this was my motto, my logo, and my refrain.

I invite you to say that with me until you believe it for yourself, no matter what your situation, no matter what the circumstance, no matter how difficult it may look just say: Lord I trust You (to be my help). Lord I trust You (to make this situation turn around). Lord I trust You (because no one else can heal this whole in my heart). Lord I trust You, (to restore my daughter, in her mind, body, soul and spirit), Lord I will trust You!

May the love of God and the sweet communion of the Holy Spirit be with you now, hence and forevermore. I commit you to him who knows the secrets of your heart and can hear those unspoken yearnings of your soul, and I ask that our Father will reveal himself to you during this your time of great need as you search for him with all your heart.

Feel the love and this great big bear hug is just for you!

Scriptures

1. When my heart is overwhelmed: lead me to the rock that's higher than I. Psalm 61:2 (KJV)

2. No one really knows what is going to happen; no one can predict the future. Ecclesiastes 10:14 (NLT)

3. Be careful for nothing; but in everything by prayer and supplication with thanksgiving let your requests be made known unto God. And the peace of God, which passeth all understanding, shall keep your hearts and minds through Christ Jesus. Philippians 4:6-7 (KJV)

4. For the Lord God will help me, therefore shall I not be confounded; therefore have I set my face like a flint, and I know that I shall not be ashamed. Isaiah 50:7 (KJV)

5. My grace is sufficient for you, for my strength is made perfect in weakness. 2 Corinthians 12:9 (KJV)

6. A new heart also will I give you, and a new spirit will I put within you: and I will take away the stony heart out of your flesh, and I will give you an heart of flesh. Ezekiel 36:26 KJV)

7. I acknowledged my sin to you and did not cover up my iniquity; I said, "I will confess my transgressions to the Lord, and you forgave the iniquity of my sin." Psalm 32:5 (ESV)

8. For the Lord God will help me, therefore shall I not be confounded; therefore have I set my face like a flint, and I know that I shall not be ashamed. Isaiah 50:7 (KJV)

9. My grace is sufficient for you, for my strength is made perfect in weakness. 2 Corinthians 12:9 (KJV)

10. A new heart also will I give you, and a new spirit will I put within you: and I will take away the stony heart out of your flesh, and I will give you an heart of flesh. Ezekiel 36:26 (KJV)I acknowledged my sin to you and did not cover up my iniquity; I said, "I will confess my transgressions to the Lord, and you forgave the iniquity of my sin." Psalm 32:5 (ESV)

11. The steadfast love of the Lord never ceases; his mercies never come to an end; they are new every morning; great is your faithfulness. Lamentations 3:22-23 (KJV)

12. And ye shall know the truth, and the truth shall make you free. John 8:32 (KJV)

13. That the trial of your faith, being much more precious than of gold that perisheth, though it be tried with fire, might be found unto praise and honour and glory at the appearing of Jesus Christ. 1 Peter 1:7 (KJV)

14. For we wrestle not against flesh and blood, but against principalities, against powers, against the rulers of darkness of this world, against spiritual wickedness in high places. Ephesians 6:12 (KJV)

15. When thou passes through the waters, I will be with thee, and through the rivers, they shall not overflow thee: when thou walkest through the fire, thou shall not be burned, neither shall the flame kindle upon thee. Isaiah 43:2 (KJV)

16. But whoso shall offend one of these little ones which believe in me, it were better for him that a millstone were hanged about his neck, and that he were drowned in the depth of the sea. Matthew 18:6 (KJV)

17. And this is the confidence that we have in him that, if we ask any thing according to his will, he heareth us. 1 John 5:14

18. For I know the plans I have for you," declares the LORD, "plans to prosper you and not to harm you, plans to give you hope and a future. Jeremiah 29:11 (NIV)

19. But my horn (emblem of excessive strength and stately grace) You have exalted like that of a wild ox; I am anointed with fresh oil. Psalm 92:10 (AMP)

20. So David went to Baal Perazim, and David defeated them there; and he said, "The LORD has broken through my enemies before me, like a breakthrough of water." 2 Samuel 5:20 (NKJV)

21. But unto you that fear my name shall the Sun of righteousness arise with healing in his wings. Malachi 4:2 (KJV)

22. Weeping may endure for a night, but joy cometh in the morning. Psalm 30:5 (KJV)

23. Some trust in chariots and some in horses, but we trust in the name of the Lord our God. Psalm 20:7 (ESV)

24. Let us not become weary in doing good, for at the proper time we will reap a harvest if we do not give up. Galatians 6:9(ESV)

25. Now, will not God bring about justice for His elect who cry to Him day and night, and will He delay long over them? I tell you that He will bring about justice for them quickly. However, when the Son of Man comes, will He find faith on the earth? Luke 18:7-8 (NASB

26. He will wipe all tears from their eyes, and there will be no more death, suffering, crying, or pain. These things of the past are gone forever. Revelation 21:4 (CEV)

27. Surely the arm of the Lord is not too short to save, nor his ear too dull to hear. Isaiah 59:1 (NIV)

28. May he strengthen your hearts so that you will be blameless and holy in the presence of our God and Father 1 Thessalonians 3:13 (NIV)

29. Make me to hear joy and gladness. Psalm 51:8 (KJV)

30. Come to me, all who labor and are heavy laden, and I will give you rest. Take my yoke upon you, and learn from me,

for I am gentle and lowly in heart, and you will find rest for your souls. For my yoke is easy, and my burden is light." Matthew 11:28-30 (ESV)

31. Thou hast turned for me my mourning into dancing: Thou hast put off my sackcloth, and girded me with gladness. Psalm 30:11 (KJV)

32. Therefore we do not lose heart. Though outwardly we are wasting away, yet inwardly we are being renewed day by day. For our light and momentary troubles are achieving for us an eternal glory that far outweighs them all. So we fix our eyes not on what is seen, but on what is unseen, since what is seen is temporary, but what is unseen is eternal. 2 Corinthians 4:16-18 (NIV)

33. A friend loveth at all times, and a brother is born for adversity. If any of you lack wisdom, let him ask of God, that giveth to all men liberally, and upbraideth not; and it shall be given him. James 1:5 (KJV)

34. I will contend with those who contend with you. Isaiah 49:25

35. Be sober, be vigilant; because your adversary the devil, as a roaring lion, walketh about, seeking whom he may devour. 1 Peter 5:8 (KJV)

36. Learn to do right! Seek justice, relieve the oppressed, and correct the oppressor. Defend the fatherless, plead for the widow. Isaiah 1:17 (AMP)

37. And God is able to bless you abundantly, so that in all things at all times, having all that you need, you will abound in every good work. 2 Corinthians 9:8 (NIV)

38. For I reckon that the sufferings of this present time are not worthy to be compared with the glory which shall be revealed in us. Romans 8:18 (NIV)

39. Now faith is confidence in what we hope for and assurance about what we do not see. Hebrews 11:1 (NIV)

40. And after you have suffered a little while, the God of all grace, who has called you to his eternal glory in Christ, will himself restore, confirm, strengthen, and establish you.1 Peter 5:10 (ESV)

41. To appoint unto them that mourn in Zion, to give unto them beauty for ashes, the oil of joy for mourning, the garment of praise for the spirit of heaviness; that they might be called trees of righteousness, the planting of the Lord that he might be glorified. Isaiah 61:3 (KJV)

42. For the eyes of the LORD move to and fro throughout the earth that He may strongly support those whose heart is completely His. 2 Chronicles 16:9 (NASB)

43. You will forget your misery; you will remember it as waters that have passed away. Job 11:16 ESV

Resources

Books:

- "A Grace Disguised," Gerald Sittser
- "Courage to Heal," Ellen Bass & Laura Davis
- "Do you have a Secret?" Jennifer Moore-Mallinos
- "Forgiving the Unforgivable," David Stoop. PhD
- "Moving Forward: Six Steps to Forgiving Yourself and Breaking Free from the Past." Everett L Worthington, Jr.
- "On the Threshold of Hope," Diane Langberg, PHD
- "Predators and Child Molesters: What Every Parent Needs to Know to Keep Kids Safe: A Sex Crimes DA Answers 100 of the Most Asked Questions," Robin Sax
- "Predators: Pedophiles, Rapists, and Other Sex Offenders," Anna C. Salter
- "Sin Against the Innocents-Sexual Abuse by the," Thomas G. Plante
- "Sistafaith: Real Stories of Pain, Truth, and Triumph," Marilyn Griffith
- "Surviving Abuse: A Journey to Forgiveness," Marie Cook
- "The Gift of Forgiveness," Eva Gibson

- "When Your Child Has Been Molested, A Parent's Guide to Healing and Recovery," Kathryn Brohl with Joyce Case Potter
- "Your Body Belongs to You," Cornelia Spellman

Web sites:

- After Silence: www.afterSilence.org
- Child Help: www.childhelp.org
- Daily Strength: www.Dailystrength.org
- Darkness to Light: www.d2l.org
- Making Daughters Safe Again: www.MDSA-online.org
- MaleSurvivor.org: www.malesurvivor.org
- Mother of Sexually Abused Children: www.MOSAC.net
- National Sex Offender Public Website: www.NSOPW.gov
- Pandora's Project: www.pandorasproject.org.uk
- Rape Abuse Incest National Network: www.RAINN.org
- StopSexOffenders.com: www.stopsexoffenders.com
- They Don't Tell: www.Theydonttell.com

Hotlines:

- Jacob Wetterling Resource Center:
  - 800-325-HOPE
  - 800-325-4673 or 651-714-4673
  - www.jwrc.org
- National Center for Missing and Exploited Children:
  - 800-THE-LOST or
  - 800-843-5678
  - www.missingkids.com
- National Suicide Prevention Hotline: (800) 273-TALK

- Stop It Now! Minnesota:
  - www.stopitnow.com/mn
  - 651-644-8515
  - www.stopitnowmn@projectpathfinder.org

Contact Us:

Website: www.LisaRGray.com

Email: Kidsdonttell@gmail.com

Facebook: They Dont Tell

(Please go on Facebook and like us)